Cambridge Elements

Elements in Philosophy of Law
edited by
George Pavlakos
University of Glasgow
Gerald J. Postema
University of North Carolina at Chapel Hill
Kenneth M. Ehrenberg
University of Surrey

THE METAPHYSICS OF LEGAL FACTS

Samuele Chilovi
Institute of Philosophy (IFS), Spanish National Research Council (CSIC)

CAMBRIDGE
UNIVERSITY PRESS

Shaftesbury Road, Cambridge CB2 8EA, United Kingdom

One Liberty Plaza, 20th Floor, New York, NY 10006, USA

477 Williamstown Road, Port Melbourne, VIC 3207, Australia

314–321, 3rd Floor, Plot 3, Splendor Forum, Jasola District Centre, New Delhi – 110025, India

103 Penang Road, #05–06/07, Visioncrest Commercial, Singapore 238467

Cambridge University Press is part of Cambridge University Press & Assessment, a department of the University of Cambridge.

We share the University's mission to contribute to society through the pursuit of education, learning and research at the highest international levels of excellence.

www.cambridge.org
Information on this title: www.cambridge.org/9781009578844

DOI: 10.1017/9781009000536

© Samuele Chilovi 2025

This publication is in copyright. Subject to statutory exception and to the provisions of relevant collective licensing agreements, with the exception of the Creative Commons version the link for which is provided below, no reproduction of any part may take place without the written permission of Cambridge University Press & Assessment.

An online version of this work is published at doi.org/10.1017/9781009000536 under a Creative Commons Open Access license CC-BY-NC 4.0 which permits re-use, distribution and reproduction in any medium for non-commercial purposes providing appropriate credit to the original work is given and any changes made are indicated. To view a copy of this license visit https://creativecommons.org/licenses/by-nc/4.0

When citing this work, please include a reference to the DOI 10.1017/9781009000536

First published 2025

A catalogue record for this publication is available from the British Library

ISBN 978-1-009-57884-4 Hardback
ISBN 978-1-009-00968-3 Paperback
ISSN 2631-5815 (online)
ISSN 2631-5807 (print)

Cambridge University Press & Assessment has no responsibility for the persistence or accuracy of URLs for external or third-party internet websites referred to in this publication and does not guarantee that any content on such websites is, or will remain, accurate or appropriate.

For EU product safety concerns, contact us at Calle de José Abascal, 56, 1°, 28003 Madrid, Spain, or email eugpsr@cambridge.org

The Metaphysics of Legal Facts

Elements in Philosophy of Law

DOI: 10.1017/9781009000536
First published online: September 2025

Samuele Chilovi
Institute of Philosophy (IFS), Spanish National Research Council (CSIC)
Author for correspondence: Samuele Chilovi, samuele.chilovi@gmail.com

Abstract: This Element tackles the question of how – in what way, and in virtue of what – facts about the legal properties and relations of particulars (such as their rights, duties, powers, etc.) are metaphysically explained. This question is divided into two separate issues. First, the Element focuses on the nature of the explanatory relation connecting legal facts to their metaphysical determinants. Second, it looks into the kinds of entities that figure in the explanation of legal facts. In doing so, it pays special attention to the role that laws, or legal norms, play in such explanations. As it turns out, there are different ways in which legal facts might be explained, all of which have something to be said in their favor, and none of which is immune from problems. This title is also available as Open Access on Cambridge Core.

Keywords: legal philosophy, social metaphysics, legal facts, legal norms, metaphysical grounding

© Samuele Chilovi 2025

ISBNs: 9781009578844 (HB), 9781009009683 (PB), 9781009000536 (OC)
ISSNs: 2631-5815 (online), 2631-5807 (print)

Contents

1 Introduction: Target and Questions　　1

2 How Are Legal Facts Explained?　　5

3 What Explains Legal Facts?　　18

4 Conclusion　　59

References　　60

1 Introduction: Target and Questions

This Element deals with a question that can roughly be put by asking how – in what way, and in virtue of what – the prelegal world is imbued with its legal aspects. The legal aspects of the world are central to the way we conduct our lives and to who we are. They bestow on us rights and obligations, powers and permissions. They allow us to play significant roles, turning us into students and professors, judges and legislators. They make us guilty and innocent, negligent and responsible. And so on. A world devoid of its legal dimension would be altered beyond recognition.

Yet while legal features are pervasive, significant, and familiar from day-to-day experience, we lack an account of how particular individuals – human and nonhuman animals, material objects, particular actions and mental states, and so on – come to possess them. Much of the literature on general jurisprudence has focused on the question of the nature of law, on what law is and how it is determined. But these questions are different from the question of how particulars instantiate the legal properties and relations that they do. And although the latter question has received little attention, it is no less central or significant.

For one thing, some are skeptical that an entity called "law" even exists,[1] yet no one would deny that individuals bear legal properties and stand in legal relations, such as legal rights and obligations.[2] At the end of the day, it might be thought, what matters is not whether there's any such thing as law but rather which properties individuals do or do not possess. Am *I* guilty? Do *we* have the rights we claim to have? These are pivotal questions, and they are questions that we'd still need to answer even if the law turned out to be a chimera fueled by philosophical speculation.

For another, if both law and legal particulars exist, we'd want to know how they are related. Do laws play a role in explaining legal particulars? And, if so, how? Without an account of how particular items instantiate legal properties and relations, and of the role of law in this process, we cannot hope to have a complete picture of legal reality.

---

[1] See, e.g., Kornhauser (ms) for a form of eliminativism about law, as well as Nye (2022, 2024) and Murphy (2008, 2014) for discussion. In Section 3.9 (see also fns. 101 and 103) I will present explanatory models of particular legal facts that do away with law.

[2] Some think that there are no distinctively legal relations (rights, obligations, etc.) because they take such relations to be moral, and therefore not to constitute a separate normative domain (see, e.g., Dworkin's "Model of Rules II" and "Hard Cases," both reprinted in Dworkin 1977; see also Dworkin 2011; Greenberg 2014; Hershovitz 2023; Stavropoulos 2021). However, such positions need not be taken to deny that legal relations exist, but can instead be understood as making a claim about their nature. Barring a radical form of eliminativism on which there are no legal properties or relations at all, the questions addressed here can be raised regardless of one's preferred view of the normativity of legal rights and obligations.

In order to get clearer on the questions we aim to address, let us introduce some terminology. Let us reserve the expression "particular legal fact" – or "legal fact" or "legal particular" – to denote facts about the instantiation of legal properties and relations by particular items.[3] Importantly, in my use of the phrase, 'legal fact' does not pick out facts about the content of the law or legal norms. Although the latter usage is common in the literature, it will not be followed here.[4]

The first data point that we need to accommodate is that no legal particular is brute or basic. Whenever a particular legal fact obtains, there is always a *reason why* it does – something that *explains why* the item in question bears the legal property or stands in the relation that it does.

Consider some examples. Esther has the right to vote in US elections. Marta has an obligation to vote in Argentinian elections. Robin and Andrea are legally married. Document *d* is a valid will. Maggie's act of driving at 70 miles per hour on Main St. was illegal. Plausibly, none of these facts – or any other fact of the same type – is explanatorily basic: they all admit of explanation. Robin and Andrea are legally married because they uttered certain words in a certain context, filled out the relevant paperwork, and so on. Esther has the right to vote in virtue of being an eighteen-year-old US citizen. What makes document *d* a valid will is that *d* was made in writing, that it was produced voluntarily by a testator with a certain age and the right state of mind, that it was signed in front of a witness. And so on.

In each of these cases, the instantiation of a legal property (or relation) is explained by the satisfaction of some underlying conditions (uttering certain words, having a certain age, etc.). What conditions? As a general matter, presumably those that, according to some law, are relevant to the instantiation of the target legal property (or relation). Since we'll be concerned here with the question of how particular legal facts are related to the satisfaction of the underlying conditions that explain them, let us also introduce some terminology to denote facts about the latter.

Let us label as "base fact" any fact about the instantiation of properties or relations that, according to some law, is relevant to the instantiation of a legal property or relation.[5] If, say, the law says that eighteen-year-old US citizens

---

[3] Some writing conventions: I use single quotation marks (e.g., 'law') to mention linguistic items, and double quotation marks (e.g., "law") to quote others' texts, for scare quotes, and to introduce new terminology.
[4] The use of 'legal fact' to refer to facts about legal content was introduced by Greenberg (2004, 2006). Others have followed him in this (see, e.g., Chilovi 2020; Chilovi and Pavlakos 2019, 2022; Chilovi and Wodak 2022; Plunkett 2012; Plunkett and Shapiro 2017).
[5] Alternatively, if one rejects the existence of laws or legal norms (see Model 0 at Section 3.9), base facts are the facts that are relevant to the instantiation of a legal property or relation. See Section 2 for how the notion of relevance should be cashed out.

have the right to vote in US elections, then facts about the instantiation of the properties *being eighteen years old* and *being a US citizen* are base facts. If the law establishes that saying certain words and filling out certain forms makes two people married, then facts about the sayings of such words and the filling outs of such forms are base facts.

The notions of a particular legal fact and of a base fact are not mutually exclusive: oftentimes, legal properties (or relations) are relevant to the instantiation of other legal properties (or relations), so that some particular legal facts will also be base facts. The fact that Esther is a US citizen, for instance, is both a particular legal fact and a base fact with respect to other legal particulars.

Our starting question can now be stated more precisely, by dividing it into two separate issues. The first concerns the nature of the *relation* that holds between particular legal facts and base facts. What are we saying when we say that Esther has the right to vote *in virtue of* being an eighteen-year-old US citizen, or that the will is valid *because* it was produced in a certain way, or that fulfilling the relevant procedure *made* Robin and Andrea legally married? It seems plausible that the relation in question must be some kind of explanatory relation, as is signaled by the explanatory locutions we use in referring to it. Yet, beyond this, it is unclear what this relation is or how it is best characterized. Section 2 is devoted to tackling this question.

The second issue, taken up in Section 3, is whether the base facts *exhaust* the kinds of entities that are responsible for explaining particular legal facts. Do they do all the explanatory work on their own or do they combine with additional elements in order to fulfill this role? If the latter, then what else figures along with them in full legal explanations? In dealing with these questions, we'll explore a variety of issues concerning laws' content and logical form, as well as legal facts' internal structure and their modal and temporal profile.

The issues addressed here are structurally analogous to ones that emerge in the social and moral realms, where similar questions arise regarding the explanation of particular social and moral facts, and about the content, form, and explanatory role of the relevant standards (social rules and moral principles). For this reason, the literature on social ontology and metaethics will be useful for dealing with the legal case,[6] although some disanalogies will become apparent, with problems arising in one case but not the others, and strategies and solutions being available here but not there.

---

[6] See, e.g., Berker (2019), Enoch (2019), Epstein (2015), Rosen (2017a, 2017b), and Schaffer (2019).

Consider the moral case. First, there are local questions in applied ethics concerning what the moral facts are in certain areas or in particular cases (What ought one do on a particular occasion?). Second, there are questions in normative ethics concerning what, in general terms, determines the moral facts (Are they grounded in the promotion of the good, the satisfaction of deontological principles, the pursuit of virtue, the balance of reasons?). Third, there are metaphysical questions about the existence and nature of moral facts and principles (Are there any? Are they mind-independent?), and about the structure of moral explanations (What is the nature of the relation between moral facts and principles, and between these and their determinants, if any? Are moral facts explained by moral principles and, if so, how?).

Similarly for the legal case. First, there are local legal questions, typically taken up by citizens and lawyers, concerning what the legal facts are in particular cases, and what the norms of the system say about certain matters. Second, there are questions in general jurisprudence regarding the nature and determination of legal norms and relations (Are legal norms determined by social facts alone or by morality as well? Are legal norms and relations – rights, duties, powers, . . . – moral?). Third, there are metaphysical questions about the structure of legal explanations (What is the nature of the relation between legal facts and norms, and between these and their determinants? Are legal facts explained by legal norms and, if so, how?).

This Element takes up questions from the last group, which are different from the issues addressed by positivist and nonpositivist theories of law. While those theories focus on the determinants of legal norms (or of facts about the content of the law), with positivists holding that they are ultimately determined by social facts, and nonpositivists maintaining that they also depend on morality,[7] our topics here differ in two important respects. First, the object of our inquiry is different, since we are concerned with the explanation of legal particulars, rather than legal norms (or legal content). Second, whereas positivist and nonpositivist theories explore the nature of the entities that do the explaining (such as whether they are social or moral in character), our focus is on structural aspects of the explanation of legal facts. (A separate Element deals with structural aspects of the explanation of legal norms.) Similarly, the issues discussed here are distinct from broader questions concerning the "normativity of law." It is not directly relevant to our present inquiry whether the law provides "robust" reasons for compliance or possesses merely "formal"

---

[7] On characterizations of positivism and nonpositivism along these lines, see, e.g., Chilovi and Pavlakos (2019), Greenberg (2004), Plunkett (2012), and Shapiro (2011). For discussion, see Tripkovic and Patterson (2023).

normativity, and different conceptions of the normativity of legal relations (rights, obligations, powers, etc.) can be paired with each of the models we will present.[8]

That said, while the issues addressed here are orthogonal to those tackled by views of general jurisprudence, as any of the models explored here can be combined with any of those views, they are not entirely unrelated. For one thing, although particular legal facts are worth targeting as an object of inquiry in their own right, doing so will illuminate our understanding of some aspects of legal norms, such as their logical form and internal structure. For another, the various elements that are involved in legal explanations – legal facts, norms, and their determinants – are intimately interconnected, since one's view about the determinants of legal norms will bear on the content of those norms, and consequently on which legal facts obtain. Questions about the explanation of legal facts and norms turn out to be complementary and indispensable aspects of a unified legal metaphysics.

2 How Are Legal Facts Explained?

Consider again our illustrative starting point:

(1) Esther has the right to vote in US elections in virtue of being an eighteen-year-old US citizen.

Sentence (1) makes an explanatory claim.[9] It provides a plausible answer to one sort of 'why'-question we can ask when we ask why Esther has the right to vote in US elections, by stating that Esther's age and citizenship are what explains why she does.

Our current question is: What kind of relation is expressed by 'in virtue of,' and cognate expressions, in claims such as (1)? Before we begin, notice two preliminary points. First, the relata of the relation we are interested in are not epistemic facts, such as the fact that one knows that Esther has the right to vote,

---

[8] There are correlations between views of the grounds and views of the normativity of law. Positivists typically argue that law possesses a type of normativity sometimes referred to as "formal." On this view, the law is normative in a weak sense: it establishes standards of correctness that can be followed or violated, but the reasons it provides for compliance are only contingently robust, depending on the moral merits the law happens to have. Nonpositivists, on the other hand, usually contend that the law has the stronger form of normativity linked to morality and sometimes referred to as "robust." For further discussion of the distinction between formal and robust normativity, see Chilovi (2024), McPherson (2018), McPherson and Plunkett (2017; 2024; in press), Plunkett, Shapiro, and Toh (2019), and Wodak (2019).
[9] Strictly speaking, (1) is shorthand for a more complex claim, since the factors that explain one's right to vote go beyond one's age and citizenship. However, for the sake of simplicity, I shall often use claims such as (1) as abbreviations of the longer, more complex ones, just to make clear what our subject matter is. The reader is invited to fill in the missing details and read my subsequent discussion in light of these additions.

or that she has a certain citizenship and age. Rather, they are the facts [Esther has the right to vote in US elections] and [Esther is an eighteen-year-old US citizen] themselves.[10] We are interested, at least primarily, in legal reality itself, rather than in how we know it.

Second, the facts of interest here are also not, at least primarily, semantic facts about the meaning of the linguistic expressions that we use to signify such reality ('right,' 'vote,' and so on). It might eventually turn out that there is some deep connection between the part of reality we are focusing on and the language we use to refer to it. But even if that were the case, it would be methodologically unwise to make legal language the target of our inquiry from the outset, since that conclusion would have to be established first.

In what follows, I outline the main candidates for capturing the 'in virtue of' relation at play in (1), namely causation, supervenience, necessitation, and metaphysical grounding. I will argue that causation, supervenience, and necessitation suffer from various problems, and that grounding enjoys several advantages over them. As a result, I will devote the second half of this section to introducing the notion of ground in more detail, and to summarizing the main features of it that will play an important role in this Element.

2.1 Causation

What, then, is the notion at work in (1)? An initial possibility might be to understand it as a causal relation. That is, to interpret (1) as:

(1c) [Esther has the right to vote in US elections] is caused by [Esther is an eighteen-year-old US citizen].

Causation is one of a handful of explanatory relations that encode the idea of one or more things accounting for, or giving rise to, something else. For this reason, it can be expressed by phrases such as 'making,' 'because,' 'in virtue of,' and 'explain,' as in 'The blossoming of the cherry tree made him joyful that day,' 'The gathering took place because we wanted to celebrate,' 'The fact that Jude helped Amy explains the fact that she was grateful to him,' and similar examples. Due to its explanatory nature, causation has several formal features that are commonly associated with explanation: controversial cases aside, it is thought to be irreflexive (nothing causes itself), asymmetric (if c causes e, then e does not cause c), and transitive (if c causes e, and e causes f, then c causes f).

Nevertheless, the idea that causation is our target relation faces various problems. First, according to some prominent accounts, the holding of

---

[10] I write '[Esther is an eighteen-year-old US citizen]' as shorthand for the conjunctive fact [Esther is eighteen years old ∧ Esther is a US citizen].

a causal relation between cause and effect either consists in or at least requires energy transfer between them (see, e.g., Castañeda 1984; Fair 1979), which is obviously absent in the case of the relation between legal facts and base facts.

Second, causation is a diachronic relation, with causes (typically) preceding their effects in time: the blossoming of the tree precedes the joy it causes, the desire to celebrate precedes the gathering taking place, Jude's helping Amy precedes Amy's gratitude toward him, and so on.[11] But now consider the instant t at which Esther, a US citizen, turns eighteen. It is not as if Esther needs to wait until *after t* in order to acquire the right to vote in elections. Rather, the time at which she becomes an eighteen-year-old US citizen is the very time at which she acquires the right to vote. To dramatize the point, if the polling station were to remain open just until t, she should still be able to cast her vote. Similarly, at each later time, t', it is the fact that Esther is at least eighteen years old and a US citizen *at t'* that determines that she has the right to vote at t'. So the relation we're looking for should at least be able to hold synchronically.[12]

This temporal discrepancy is a symptom of a deeper divergence between ways in which things can be "brought about," or "determined," by other things. Causal determination is one way in which some facts or events can bring about or give rise to others. Yet when Esther's age and citizenship together combine to make it the case that she has the right to vote, her right is generated by these other properties in a different way: it is *constitutively* determined by them.

To see the contrast between constitutive and causal determination, consider two phenomena that are both generated by human affairs, but in very different ways. On the one hand, consider climate change. Climate change is clearly partly a product of human activities, in the sense that it is caused by them. However, climate change is not determined by humans in the sense of being constituted by them. This becomes evident when we ask what climate change is. For, albeit caused by humans, climate change is nevertheless a natural phenomenon as it consists of natural processes and events describable in purely physical terms, without reference to humans.

On the other hand, consider the property of being popular. This property is also, in a sense, the product of human affairs: it is the way that people regard other people (or things) that determines whether someone (or something) is popular. But the sense in which someone's being popular is a function of facts about us is quite different. For it is not as if people's attitudes and responses caused someone to be popular, as if by dressing them up somehow. Rather, for someone to be popular *just is* for them to be regarded in certain ways by other

---

[11] See, e.g., Davidson (1967).
[12] In Section 3.7.2, we'll examine ways in which one may challenge the view that this relation always holds synchronically.

people: this is what being popular is or consists in. As before, there is a temporal component to this. Once the (extrinsic) conditions for being popular have been met, it is not as if one needs to wait in order to instantiate the property of being popular. Rather, at each time t when someone satisfies the conditions for being popular, that determines that they *are* popular at t.

For a case that manifests the contrast between constitutive and causal determination in relation to the same *explanandum*, consider the question of what makes a certain wall white.[13] If we were asking the causal question, the answer would presumably appeal to past facts about the wall, leading up to it being painted white, and the explanation would thereby be diachronic. If we were asking the constitutive question, the answer, by contrast, would appeal to things such as the reflectance profile of the surface, the surface's disposition to appear in certain ways to perceivers under normal conditions and the like (depending on one's metaphysics of color), and the explanation would be synchronic.

These examples should serve to highlight the distinction between constitutive and causal determination, and serve as a comparison with the legal case that interests us here. Just as Esther's being popular is constitutively determined by underlying facts about collective mental states, and the surface's color is determined by its categorical or dispositional features, Esther's right to vote constitutively depends, given US law on the matter, on her age and citizenship. Naturally, these cases are different in many other respects since they involve different relata, but they are similar in how they are determined by the underlying facts.

2.2 Supervenience and Necessitation

Granting that the 'in virtue of' relation expressed by (1) is not causation, another possibility might be to understand it in modal terms. One option here would be to cash out (1) as a necessitation claim to the effect that the fact that Esther is an eighteen-year-old US citizen necessitates the fact that she has the right to vote:[14]

(1n) Necessarily, if [Esther is an eighteen-year-old US citizen] obtains, then [Esther has the right to vote in US elections] obtains.

Likewise, another possible modal interpretation would be to cash out (1) as a supervenience claim, to the effect that [Esther has the right to vote in US elections] supervenes on [Esther is an eighteen-year-old US citizen]:[15]

---

[13] Thanks to Mark Greenberg for suggesting this example.
[14] In general, a set of facts Γ necessitates a fact [p] iff necessarily, if every member of Γ obtains, then so does [p].
[15] In general, a set of facts Δ supervenes on a set of facts Γ iff any worlds that are Γ-indiscernible are Δ-indiscernible. Two worlds are Γ-indiscernible iff they agree on the obtaining of every fact [p] ∈ Γ, i.e., if each member of Γ either obtains at both worlds or obtains at neither.

(1s) For any two possible worlds w, w': if w, w' agree on whether [Esther is an eighteen-year-old US citizen] obtains, then w, w' agree on whether [Esther has the right to vote in US elections] obtains,

where two worlds agree on whether [p] obtains iff either [p] obtains at both worlds or it obtains at neither.

Supervenience and necessitation have been used to formulate a wide range of determination theses in the philosophy of mind, language, and epistemology, including physicalism, dualism, and a variety of internalist and externalist theses.[16] Yet the project of interpreting 'in virtue of' claims as supervenience or necessitation claims faces serious challenges, some inherent to their use in the legal case, and others more general in character.

Let us start with the specific challenges inherent to the legal case. One problem is that, on the usual interpretation that supervenience and necessitation claims are given, claims such as (1n) and (1s) are false. Since the modality within them is typically understood as metaphysical modality, (1n) implies that it is absolutely impossible for Esther to be an eighteen-year-old US citizen without having the right to vote, and (1s) implies that it is impossible for Esther's voting rights to change without a change in her age or citizenship. But this seems clearly false. Since the laws governing voting rights are contingent[17] – they could be, and could have been, different – there are situations (say, the actual world) where Esther is both an eighteen-year-old US citizen and can vote in elections, and there are also possible situations where she's an eighteen-year-old US citizen and yet she can't vote – say, because the minimum voting age is set at twenty-one.

One way to fix this problem would be to restrict the modality in (1n) and (1s). In this vein, the scope of (1n) and (1s) could be interpreted as limited to worlds where US voting laws are as they actually are. If we only look at worlds where US law is such that all and only eighteen-year-old US citizens have the right to vote, any two people who have the same age and citizenship will be alike as to whether they can vote, and so in particular [Esther has the right to vote] will supervene on, and be necessitated by, [Esther is an eighteen-year-old US citizen] within this set of worlds.

---

[16] See, e.g., Chalmers (1996), Jackson (1998), and Lewis (1983, 1994) for formulations of physicalism as supervenience or necessitation claims. For formulations of semantic internalism and externalism as supervenience claims, see, e.g., Kallestrup (2012) and Haukioja (2017). For formulations of internalism and externalism about epistemic justification in terms of supervenience, see, e.g., Srinivasan (2020).

[17] Even natural law theorists who believe that some legal norms are metaphysically necessary moral principles presumably countenance some laws that are not, so this problem will emerge even within their framework.

Even this amended version, however, is liable to serious objections. One problem is that the truth of (1n) and (1s) is compatible with their converses also being true. In general, necessitation and supervenience are not asymmetric relations, and so they can run in both directions. Explanation, by contrast, is asymmetric: if x explains y, in the relevant sense, then y cannot explain x, since circular explanations are vicious.

But the problem here runs even deeper. For it's not just that (1n) and (1s) leave open that their converses might be true. Rather, their converses *are* true: all worlds (with the same laws as actuality) where Esther has the right to vote in US elections are worlds where she is at least eighteen years old and a US citizen: she couldn't have that right without having that age and citizenship; and any two worlds (with the same laws as actuality) that agree on whether Esther has the right to vote must also agree on whether she is at least eighteen years old and a US citizen. Therefore this is a case in which supervenience and necessitation run in both directions. But then, if the restricted version of supervenience or necessitation yielded apt regimentations of 'in virtue of' claims, we should also say that Esther is at least eighteen years old and a US citizen in virtue of having the right to vote, which is clearly false.

More generally, it is by now widely accepted that supervenience and necessitation do not adequately capture the notion of determination or dependence that is at work in claims such as (1), for two sorts of reasons.[18] One problem is that supervenience and necessitation have different formal properties than those that are generally thought to be possessed by the target notion of determination or dependence.[19] First, supervenience and necessitation are reflexive relations, meaning that they hold between anything and itself: for any x, x is necessitated by and supervenes on x. Second, as witnessed by the case involving Esther, they are not asymmetric: x being necessitated by or supervening on y does not rule out y likewise being necessitated by or supervening on x.[20] Third, they are monotonic relations, meaning that supervenience and necessitation bases can be arbitrarily expanded *salva veritate*: if x is necessitated by or supervenes on y, then, similarly, x is necessitated by or supervenes on y together with anything else.

Determination and dependence, by contrast, are often thought to have different logical features. They are irreflexive: nothing depends on or is determined by itself. They are asymmetric: if x depends on and is determined by y, then

---

[18] I take 'determination' and 'dependence' to be converses of one another: x determines y if and only if (iff) y depends on x.

[19] The argument from formal properties is given, inter alia, by Koslicki (2015: 308), Leuenberger (2014a: 228), McLaughlin and Bennett (2021: §3.5), Raven (2012: 690; 2013: 194), and Schaffer (2009: 364).

[20] They are neither symmetric nor asymmetric: sometimes they hold symmetrically (as in reflexive cases), and sometimes they hold asymmetrically.

y does not depend on and is not determined by *x*. And they are nonmonotonic, so that it is not the case that if *x* depends on and is determined by *y*, then *x* depends on and is determined by *y* together with anything else.

That said, for two main reasons it is unclear whether this argument is ultimately compelling. First, it is not entirely clear that determination and dependence really do have the formal properties that the argument ascribes to them. One way of establishing that they do would be by showing that determination and dependence *inherit* these properties from other relations to which they are closely connected, and especially from explanation and relative fundamentality, both of which are irreflexive, asymmetric, and nonmonotonic.[21] However, it is an open question how determination and dependence are related to these other notions, and so it is an open question whether it shares such properties with them.[22]

The second reason why the argument is not conclusive is that, even if determination and dependence do have these properties, it might still be possible to define them in terms of supervenience (or necessitation), by appealing to *one-way* supervenience (see Berker 2018: 736; Kovacs 2019). To illustrate, say that a set Γ *one-way* supervenes on a set Δ iff (i) Γ supervenes on Δ; (ii) Δ does not supervene on Γ; and (iii) Γ does not supervene on any proper subset of Δ. Then we would have introduced a supervenience relation that is both asymmetric (and hence irreflexive) and nonmonotonic, thus possessing the desired formal features.

However, a second line of argument has proven more resilient. The central problem is that one of the key features of determination is that, unlike intensional notions such as supervenience and necessitation, it is *hyperintensional*. This means that it can fail to hold between cointensional (i.e., necessarily coextensive) entities, and that it can fail to hold under substitution of necessary equivalents.

This key difference underlies the fact that modal accounts of constitutive determination systematically overgenerate by producing many *false positives*. That is, cases of entities that are related by supervenience or necessitation but where no determination relation holds.

---

[21] That is, explanation and relative fundamentality are subject to the following principles. Irreflexivity: Nothing explains or is more fundamental than itself. Asymmetry: If *x* explains or is more fundamental than *y*, then *y* respectively does not explain or is not more fundamental than *x*. Nonmonotonicity: It is not the case that if *x* explains or is more fundamental than *y*, then the collection of *x* together with an arbitrary entity *z* likewise explains or is more fundamental than *y*.

[22] See, e.g., Trogdon (2013a: 106) for the claim that grounding inherits irreflexivity from explanation, and Dasgupta (2014a: 4), Rosen (2010: 116), and Trogdon (2013a: 109) for a similar claim with regard to nonmonotonicity. For a critical discussion of the argument from inheritance in the context of the relation between grounding and explanation, see Maurin (2019).

First, necessary entities one-way supervene on many things they do not depend on. For a trivial example, [2 + 2 = 4] one-way supervenes on the fact that I'm sitting: any two worlds that agree on whether I'm sitting also agree on [2 + 2 = 4] (and not *vice versa*), simply because they must agree that [2 + 2 = 4] obtains.

Second, following Fine's (1994, 1995) popular example, consider Socrates and {Socrates}, the set whose sole member is Socrates.[23] Given standard assumptions in set theory, [Socrates exist] and [{Socrates} exists] are cointensional: any world where Socrates exists is a world where {Socrates} does, and vice versa. So [Socrates exists] and [{Socrates} exists] supervene on, and necessitate, each other. Yet it is plausible that while {Socrates} exists because Socrates does, the converse is not true. Therefore, while the determination and the dependence each run in *one* direction, with the existence of {Socrates} determined by and depending on the existence of Socrates, the necessitation and the supervenience run in *both* directions. And this gives rise to another false positive: [Socrates exists] supervenes on and is necessitated by [{Socrates} exists], without being determined by it. At the same time, trying to solve this problem by using the notion of one-way supervenience would yield a *false negative*. For, by hypothesis, [{Socrates} exists] *is* determined by [Socrates exists], yet the former fails to one-way supervene on the latter, since the supervenience runs in both directions.[24] So, in general, cases of determination between cointensional entities generate false positives for supervenience, and false negatives for one-way supervenience.

Other cases of this sort are not hard to find. For one, consider truths and their truthmakers. For example, [grass is green] and [<grass is green> is true][25] are cointensional: wherever grass is green, the proposition that grass is green is true, and vice versa. Yet it is grass being green that makes the proposition <grass is green> true, not the other way round. And one-way supervenience fails to hold.

For another, some cases involving legal particulars and base facts are also of this kind. As we noticed, [Esther has the right to vote in US elections] and [Esther is an eighteen-year-old US citizen] are cointensional relative to worlds that share the same voting laws as the present-day United States. Yet it is the former fact that holds in virtue of the latter, not vice versa. And one-way supervenience fails to hold.

---

[23] As noted by Berker (2018), similar arguments against identifying determination with supervenience had previously been advanced by Dancy (1981) and DePaul (1987) in the case of ethical properties.

[24] That is, if we understand determination/dependence as one-way supervenience, then we cannot say that [{Socrates} exists] is determined by [Socrates exists], since the two facts supervene on each other and so the former does not one-way supervene on the latter.

[25] As is customary, '<*p*>' reads: 'the proposition that *p*.'

What the foregoing points suggest is that analyzing the target notion of determination in causal or modal terms won't work. For this and related reasons, in recent years an increasing number of philosophers have started to theorize about determination directly, rather than trying to replace it with surrogate notions. The underlying idea behind this turn was not to introduce or engineer a novel technical concept but rather to take seriously a notion that is already present in ordinary discourse, and that has been at the core of philosophy for a long time.[26] The result has been a growing body of work dealing with the nature and logic of determination in its own right, developed under the heading of "grounding theory."[27]

2.3 Metaphysical Grounding

The notion of ground has become the locus around which the study of constitutive determination has settled. It promises to capture and regiment the idea of some things giving rise to, or accounting for, some others, where this generative link holds, typically at least, not across time, as in the case of causation, but rather across different "levels of reality" at a time. In this spirit, one may suppose that physical facts about particles ground chemical facts about molecules, which in turn determine the existence of biological organisms and (perhaps) their mental states, whose interactions generate societies and legal systems. By providing an interlevel connector, the notion of ground underwrites a conception of reality on which not everything is metaphysically on a par. Only a restricted class of entities – if any – is regarded as absolutely ungrounded and therefore fundamental,[28] whereas all others are derivative, arising from the more fundamental ones on which they depend.

Now let's go back to particular legal facts. As we noticed at the beginning, legal particulars are a clear example of derivative entities. When we wonder why someone's action has the legal status it does, it is not as if there were no answer to be had. Such facts cannot just be brute, inexplicable elements of reality. Rather, such facts must be explainable by some array of other facts. Taking grounding as our relation of choice then leads us to understand (1) as:

(1g) [Esther has the right to vote in US elections] is grounded in [Esther is an eighteen-year-old US citizen].

---

[26] Dating back at least as far as Plato's dialogues, with Euthyphro, who is inquiring into the nature of piety, posing the question: "Is an act pious *because* it is loved by the gods, or do the gods love it *because* it is pious?" On the history of grounding in ancient and modern philosophy, see Amijee (2020), Corkum (2016, 2020), Malink (2020), and Roski (2017, 2020).
[27] Starting with the work of Audi (2012), Bennett (2011), Correia (2005, 2010), Fine (2001, 2012), Rosen (2010), and Schaffer (2009).
[28] Candidate fundamentalia include the entities that figure in fundamental physics, phenomenal states, mathematical objects, and basic moral principles.

This reading of (1), however, is only as helpful and illuminating as the underlying notion of grounding it appeals to. In what follows, I set out some of the core features of grounding and outline some of the debates concerning them, placing particular emphasis on those of special relevance to the arguments to follow. In particular, it will be especially important to be aware of: (i) the relation among grounding, determination, and explanation; (ii) some key distinctions in the theory of ground (full vs. partial, mediate vs. immediate, etc.); (iii) ground's structural features (asymmetry, transitivity, etc.); and (iv) the relation between grounding and metaphysical necessity. At the end of Section 2.3.4, I'll flag the assumptions I make regarding these issues and how they bear on subsequent arguments.

2.3.1 Determination and Explanation

So far we've fluctuated between characterizing grounding as a form of determination and explanation, but these two usages in fact correspond to different conceptions of grounding. Although it is widely held that grounding is an explanatory notion, this thought can be precisified in at least two different ways, corresponding to what Raven (2015: 326) calls "unionism" and "separatism." According to unionism, the relation between grounding and (constitutive) explanation is one of identity: grounding is identical to a constitutive, objective sort of explanation.[29] According to separatism, by contrast, the relation between grounding and explanation is one of backing: grounding is a kind of worldly determination that backs, or underwrites, metaphysical explanations.[30]

Though on a separatist view grounding and explanation are distinct, there is still a tight relation between them: whenever some facts ground another, this licenses a true explanatory claim to the effect that the grounded fact obtains because its grounds do. So each ground is an explanans of what it grounds: grounds are always parts of the explanations of what they ground. Crucially, however, it is open to the separatist to deny that the converse is true: not all explanantia need to be grounds, since explanations may appeal to considerations additional to those that correspond to the facts in the grounding base. On a unionist view, by contrast, this option is foreclosed: any metaphysical explanans counts as a ground, since grounding *is* the relation of explanation that things in the explanatory base stand in (vis-à-vis what they explain). Though I will be as neutral as possible on this issue (and move back and forth between these two

---

[29] Proponents of unionism include Dasgupta (2017), Fine (2012), Litland (2015), and Rosen (2010).
[30] Advocates of separatism include Audi (2012), Schaffer (2009, 2012, 2016), and Trogdon (2013a).

conceptions when doing so is unproblematic), we will see that at some junctures it makes a significant difference to how the metaphysics of legal reality is modeled, and affords different resources to deal with various problems (see especially Section 3.6).

2.3.2 Regimentation

Another issue concerns how grounding claims are best regimented, that is, what their underlying *logical form* is. While claims of ground can take several grammatical forms in natural language (we noticed before the use of both 'because' and 'in virtue of' in English), the question here is whether there is a canonical form in which to express them: one that is most perspicuous in representing the underlying phenomenon.[31]

Several issues arise with regard to regimentation. One is whether grounding claims are best formulated with the use of a predicate expression (such as the predicate 'grounds' / 'is grounded in') denoting a relation, or rather by means of a sentential operator (such as the non-truth-functional connective 'because'). On the predicational view, a canonical grounding claim has the form '$[p]$ is grounded in $[q_1]$, $[q_2]$, ...,' or '$[p]$ is grounded in Γ,' where Γ is a collection of entities (say, facts). On the operational view, the canonical form would be 'p because $q_1, q_2, \ldots,$' or 'p because Θ,' where 'Θ' is a collection of sentences.[32]

An advantage of the operational view is its ontological neutrality since it commits neither to the existence of a relation of grounding nor to the existence of certain entities as needed to act as grounding relata. The predicational view, on the other hand, is attractive to those who conceive of grounding as a relation holding between some entities (possibly of a certain category). In this respect, some (e.g., Audi 2012; Rosen 2010) take the view that the relata of grounding must be facts, while others (e.g., Schaffer 2009, 2016), hold the liberal view that grounding can in principle relate entities drawn from any ontological category (facts, objects, actions, properties, etc.).

Regardless of which of these two regimentations is preferred, a further issue concerns the adicity of the ground-theoretic idiom of choice. It seems pretty clear that it should be possible to fill the grammatical position occupied, in a grounding statement, by the ground(s) with a plural term (as was done earlier), since something can be grounded in a plurality of things. To take a typical case

---

[31] See Correia and Schnieder (2012: 10).

[32] The view that grounding statements are best regimented with a relational predicate has been advocated by Audi (2012) and Rosen (2010). A contrastive variant of the latter view is defended by Schaffer (2012, 2016). The opposing view that they should be regimented with a non-truth-functional sentential connective has been endorsed by Correia (2010) and Fine (2012).

for illustration, the conjunctive fact $[p \wedge q]$ is grounded partly in $[p]$ and partly in $[q]$, so these two facts together ground it. The question is whether all grounding claims are like this, singular on one side and plural on the other (with the one-one case being the special case involving a degenerate plurality), or whether we should allow for many-many grounding claims, irreducibly plural on both sides.[33]

For the sake of concreteness and for ease of exposition, here I will mostly use a two-place predicational expression, flanked by a singular term on the side of what is grounded and by a plural term on the side of its ground(s), and assume the existence of a grounding relation signified by it. Furthermore, I will mostly focus on the grounding of facts, though I take it to be possible for grounding to hold between entities of other sorts too (and will sometimes speak as if it does).

2.3.3 Key Distinctions

Implicit in the idea that a plurality of facts can collectively ground another plurality of facts is an important distinction between full and partial ground. Common ways of drawing this distinction take the notion of full ground as primitive, and define partial ground in terms of it, as a part of a full ground (see, e.g., Fine 2012: 50). Specifically, a (nonempty, possibly infinite, possibly degenerate) collection of facts Γ fully grounds $[p]$ when nothing needs to be added to Γ in order for it to provide a complete account of $[p]$. And $[p]$ is partially grounded in Δ if there is some plurality Γ such that $[p]$ is fully grounded in Δ, Γ.

Notice that it is plausible that a fact may have multiple independent full grounds (Fine 2012: 47), opening the door to metaphysical overdetermination. For instance, if disjunctive facts are grounded in their true disjuncts, then $[p \vee q]$ is fully grounded in $[p]$, and also fully grounded in $[q]$, if $[p]$ and $[q]$ both obtain (see Fine 2012: 40, 51; Rosen 2010: 117).[34] Given a principle of amalgamation (Fine 2012: 57),[35] this will imply that $[p]$ and $[q]$ together also fully ground $[p \vee q]$.

Another important distinction is that between immediate and mediate grounds. A plurality Γ is an immediate ground for $[p]$ if there is no fact $[q]$ that needs to "mediate" between Γ and $[p]$, that is, no fact $[q]$ such that Γ grounds $[p]$ *via* $[q]$ (with Γ grounding $[q]$, which in turn grounds $[p]$). A mediate

---

[33] See Dasgupta (2014b) for an argument in favor of many-many grounding.
[34] For challenges to the view that true disjunctions are always made true by their true disjuncts, see López de Sa (2009).
[35] Formulated in terms of facts, amalgamation says that if a plurality Γ fully grounds $[p]$ and another (possibly nonoverlapping) plurality Δ fully grounds $[p]$, then Γ, Δ together also fully ground $[p]$.

ground of [p], by contrast, is a ground of a ground (of a ground, ...) of [p]. To take a toy example, [p] immediately grounds [p ∨ q], but only mediately grounds [(p ∨ q) ∨ r].

2.3.4 Structural Principles

Let us turn to the structural principles that govern grounding. First, the notion of ground employed here is factive: if Γ grounds [p], then all the facts in Γ as well as [p] obtain. Second, as previously noticed, grounding differs in key respects both from modal relations and from causation. Unlike supervenience and necessitation, grounding is usually taken to be explanatory, hyperintensional, nonmonotonic, and to induce a strict partial ordering over the entities in its domain (i.e., to be transitive, irreflexive, and asymmetric).[36] Unlike causation, grounding is a constitutive form of determination or explanation. As such, it is often held to be synchronic (i.e., subject to the requirement that it relate only cotemporal entities), and necessitating (i.e., subject to the principle that grounds metaphysically necessitate what they ground).[37] Applied to the grounding of facts, the latter principle amounts to the following widely held view:

> GROUNDING NECESSITARIANISM If Γ fully grounds [p], then, necessarily, if Γ obtains then [p] obtains.

In order to present the arguments that will occupy us, the foregoing illustration of grounding's features should suffice. Still, it is important to be aware that there is widespread disagreement over the exact nature of grounding, especially over whether it is irreflexive, asymmetric, transitive, synchronic, or necessitating.[38]

---

[36] Irreflexivity: Nothing grounds itself. Asymmetry: If x is a ground of y, then y is no ground of x. Transitivity: If x grounds y, and y grounds z, then x grounds z. Nonmonotonicity: It is not the case that if x grounds y, then x together with any arbitrary entity z also grounds y. Hyperintensionality: It is not the case that if x grounds y, and x is cointensional with z, then z also grounds y; and it is not the case that if x grounds y, and y is cointensional with z, then x also grounds z. Each of these features is probably accepted by most authors. See Raven (2020) for an overview of the debates over whether grounding has them.

[37] Though if GROUNDING NECESSITARIANISM holds, then grounding requires necessitation. Note that this is compatible with the point made earlier that grounding (determination/dependence) cannot be captured by necessitation since there would still be instances of necessitation without grounding. Advocates of the view that grounds necessitate what they ground include Audi (2012), Bennett (2011), Bernstein (2016), Correia (2005, 2018), Dasgupta (2014a, 2014b), deRosset (2013), Fine (2012), Litland (2017), Loss (2016, 2017), Rosen (2010), Trogdon (2013b), and Wilsch (2015). This view has been challenged, e.g., by Leuenberger (2014b) and Skiles (2015). For discussion, see Chilovi (2021) and Kovacs (2020).

[38] For challenges to the irreflexivity of grounding, see especially Jenkins (2011) and Kovacs (2018); the principle is also discussed by Fine (2010) and Krämer (2013). On asymmetry, see Bliss (2014) and Thompson (2016). On transitivity, see Litland (2013), Loss (2017), Schaffer (2012), and Tahko (2013).

For current purposes, we may divide the assumptions we have made about grounding into four main categories. First, there are those that are strictly optional to the current project. Issues of regimentation fall within this class: for the sake of definiteness, I make specific assumptions about regimentation, but one can easily do without them and say everything, or nearly everything that I say here with a different choice of assumptions. Second, there are assumptions that play an important role in the ensuing discussion, since key arguments depend on them, but which are typically shared by the various parties to the relevant disputes. The structural features of asymmetry, irreflexivity, transitivity, nonmonotonicity, explanatoriness, and hyperintensionality fall into this category. Third, there are principles, such as GROUNDING NECESSITARIANISM, that play an important role in some arguments, but which could easily be disputed by some of the relevant parties – as we will see, rejecting this principle is a crucial step in the defense of some positions from objections (see Section 3.8). And finally there are features that, in light of the discussion to follow, we may well have good reason to drop altogether since the problems they encounter are so severe that no way of rescuing them seems plausible. This may well apply to synchronicity (see Section 3.7.2).

This concludes our preliminary treatment of the nature of the relation between legal particulars and base facts. As we shall see shortly, claiming that the relation is grounding doesn't answer the question in its entirety. In order to do that, we need to inquire into the question of whether base facts are the complete explanantia of legal facts.

3 What Explains Legal Facts?

We've arrived at the preliminary conclusion that the relation between [Esther has the right to vote] and [Esther is an eighteen-year-old US citizen] is grounding. Given that [Esther is an eighteen-year-old US citizen] grounds [Esther has the right to vote], and given that each ground is an explanans of what it grounds, the former fact falls within the latter's explanatory base. Generalizing from this, given any legal particular taken as the explanandum, its explanatory base, or set of explanantia, will at least include some base facts. Which ones? On a natural line of thought, there will be some law or laws regulating the matter at hand, and establishing certain features as relevant to the acquisition of the legal property that figures in the target legal fact, so that facts about the instantiation of these features should count as the base facts that ground the target legal particular.

If this is right, then two questions immediately arise: first, is the relation between legal facts and base facts full or partial grounding? Second, do base facts exhaust the immediate explanantia of legal particulars, or should explanatory bases be supplemented with additional resources? The two questions are connected since if the relation between legal particulars and base facts is partial grounding, then surely the explanation base will need to be supplemented, and, correlatively, if base facts exhaust the explanation base, then the relation between them and legal facts must be one of full ground.

I will introduce and explore six different models of the explanation of legal facts, which divide along two main axes: first, regarding whether they appeal to laws, or general legal norms, as additional explanantia of legal particulars; and second, among models that do appeal to legal norms, regarding the kind of explanatory role that norms are assigned. Four of these models agree that legal norms play some explanatory role, but disagree on whether base facts are partial (Models 1–2) or full (Models 3–4) grounds of legal facts, and on the kind of explanatory role that legal norms have: the grounds of legal particulars (Models 1–2), the grounds of grounding facts (Model 2–3), or explanantia but not grounds (Model 4). By contrast, a fifth model (Model 5) gives up the assumption that legal norms are explanatory and conceives of them as generalizations which do not govern their instances but merely summarize them. Finally, Model 0 denies the existence of laws altogether and explains legal facts without appealing to them (see Table 1).

Before we examine these accounts, first let me clarify what I mean by 'legal norm.' Legal norms, as I understand them, are general standards that connect legal properties with the underlying properties responsible for explaining them. In so doing, they set out conditions for the obtaining of legal facts and single out a range of potential base facts (facts about the satisfaction of such conditions). The general standards that eighteen-year-old US citizens have the right to vote

Table 1 Summary of views

	LNs exist	LNs explain	LNs ground legal facts	LNs ground grounding facts	BFs partial grounds of LFs	BFs full grounds of LFs
M0	o	o	o	o	x	o
M1	x	x	x	o	x	o
M2	x	x	x	x	x	o
M3	x	x	o	x	o	x
M4	x	x	o	o	o	x
M5	x	o	o	o	o	x

Note: "LN," "BF," and "LF" abbreviate "legal norm," "base fact," and "legal fact," respectively.

in US elections and that valid wills in Scotland must be in writing and signed in front of a witness, for instance, are legal norms. Legal norms then involve three essential ingredients: some legal property or relation (a legal right, obligation, permission, status, etc.), some underlying "base" conditions (a plurality of legal or nonlegal properties or relations), and a relation between them, such that the instantiation of the former is connected to the satisfaction of the latter. What that relation is will be one of the main questions of this section.

Second, let me clarify how my use of 'legal norm' relates to cognate expressions, such as 'law,' 'a law,' and 'the law,' as well as to how our current notion of a legal norm relates to metaphysical disputes about legal norms' nature and grounds, and to the positivism–nonpositivism debate specifically. First, I take legal norms to be things that can be legally valid in legal systems.[39] And when they do become valid in a system, they become part of the law of that system. In other words, collections of legally valid norms make up a system's law: the law of a system s at a time t is the collection of norms that are legally valid in s at t.[40] Further, I use the mass noun 'law' to speak of uncountable quantities of valid legal norms, and the count noun phrase 'a law,' as well as its plural 'laws,' to speak of countable collections thereof.[41] Relatedly, legal norms are closely related to what Greenberg (2004, 2006) and others have called 'legal facts.'[42] 'Legal facts' in Greenberg's sense are facts about the content of the law (in a system, at a time), that is, facts about legal norms being legally valid. Therefore, while they are closely related to my notion of a legal norm – legal norms are constituents of Greenberg's legal facts – they are different from what I call 'legal facts' here.

Let me emphasize two further aspects of what I have just said. First, I use 'legal norms' (and 'law') to speak of legal norms of all kinds: not just the norms of statutory law but also those that form part of constitutional law and customary law, those that result from judicial precedents in systems of common law, and so on. Second, legal norms must be sharply distinguished from the sources of law, such as authoritative texts, utterances, and speech acts. The two are intimately related since legal sources are part of what makes norms legally valid when they are. However, they are distinct types of objects: while legal sources typically consist of concrete and spatiotemporally located entities, legal norms

---

[39] I use the relational predicate 'is legally valid in' as synonymous with 'is law in.' This minimal notion is meant to be available to both positivists and nonpositivists as it is neutral on the question of what the grounds of law and validity are.

[40] This raises some familiar questions. What are legal systems? Are they sets of norms, structured bodies thereof, or something else altogether? What is the relation of legal validity? Is it membership, parthood, or something else? What are the identity criteria for legal norms and systems? Luckily, for current purposes we don't need to answer these questions.

[41] In this terminological choice, I follow Shapiro (2011: ch. 1).   [42] See fn. 4.

are arguably best viewed as abstract objects. This, indeed, is reflected in their divergent modal profiles, as legal norms can survive changes that their sources cannot. (A legal source could be destroyed without the corresponding norm thereby ceasing to exist.)

Finally, our current notion of a legal norm is not committed to falling on either side of Dworkin's (1977) famous rules–principles distinction (with rules applying in an "all-or-nothing" fashion, and principles having "weight"). Some legal norms could be "rules" in Dworkin's sense, while others could be "principles," and nothing said here should preclude either of these possibilities.

Relatedly, the notion of a legal norm employed here should be equally available to positivist and nonpositivist theories of law. Positivists and nonpositivists can be viewed as disagreeing on the question of how facts about the content of the law are metaphysically explained, that is, on what makes norms legally valid. In a nutshell, while positivists believe that the validity of legal norms is ultimately explained by social facts alone, nonpositivists hold that law's ultimate determinants comprise moral facts and principles.[43] The positivism–nonpositivism debate interacts in interesting ways with the question of how particular legal facts are determined (more on this in a moment), but the first thing to notice is that both parties to this dispute accept – indeed, presuppose – the existence of legal norms in the minimal sense outlined here.

Now, the question of interest here – what explains particular legal facts – is closely tied to the question, debated by positivists and nonpositivists, of how the validity of legal norms is to be explained. First, as we've seen, legal facts are grounded, at least in part, in base facts. What facts need to obtain in order for a given legal particular to come into existence depends on what the conditions are for the instantiation of legal properties and relations encoded in legally valid norms. And what norms are legally valid depends, in turn, on how law is determined. This, indeed, is reflected in the fact that positivism and nonpositivism disagree not only at the explanatory "input" level – on what explains legal norms – but also at the extensional "output" level – on which norms are valid, on what the content of the law is. Because of the different stances they take on the prior explanatory question, they often reach different conclusions on the content of particular laws. Therefore the positivism–nonpositivism debate bears a close relation to the question of what explains particular legal facts: different legal

---

[43] For a conception and elaboration of the positivism/nonpositivism dispute along these lines, see, e.g., Atiq (2020), Berman (2018, 2021, 2024), Chilovi (2020), Chilovi and Pavlakos (2019, 2022), Chilovi and Wodak (2022), Gardner (2001), Greenberg (2004), Plunkett (2012), and Shapiro (2011). Influential advocates of positivism include Coleman (2001), Hart (1961), Leiter (2007), Marmor (2009), Moreso (2001), Raz (1979), Shapiro (2011), and Waluchow (1994). Prominent nonpositivists include Dworkin (1977, 1986), Finnis (1979), Greenberg (2014), and Stavropoulos (1996).

determinants generate laws with different content, which in turn affects the range of base facts that can ground particular legal facts.

Nevertheless, the bearing of the positivism–nonpositivism debate on our topic should not be overestimated. First, in many cases, different accounts of legal determinants reach the same conclusion regarding which norms are legally valid. These are cases where positivism and nonpositivism agree on what the law says, even if they disagree on what explains it. How widespread this agreement is is a matter of dispute, but it's doubtless that many such cases exist. Taking advantage of this, I will work mainly with cases of legal norms that both positivists and nonpositivists would presumably count as law, rather than with norms whose validity is disputed.[44] Bracketing this dispute will allow us to sharpen our focus on the question that interests us here, and to isolate it from immaterial issues.

Second, and relatedly, even in cases where the norms in question *are* disputed, this discrepancy doesn't bear on our main topic. We will be examining the questions of what explains particular legal facts, whether norms explain them, and how. In doing so, we will consider five different models of the explanation of particular legal facts that differ on the role they assign to legal norms. As I briefly mentioned in the introduction, these are structural issues that can be addressed independently of one's views of what the content of the law is, and of how it is determined. For, regardless of one's take on these issues, one can still ask whether the norms that one regards as law (and explains in the way that one favors) function as determinants of legal facts. In practice, those who doubt that the norms I use as examples are law can just substitute their own legal norms in the explanatory models and evaluate the same range of alternatives for explaining legal facts. Since every model we'll address can be combined with either positivist or nonpositivist accounts of legal norms, the positivism–nonpositivism dispute will be orthogonal to the question at hand.

So much for my conciliatory remarks. For all issues regarding the nature of legal norms that we can stay neutral on, there are also a few questions that we do need to address since they bear directly on the question of how legal facts are explained. These concern legal norms' logical form, and their modal and temporal profile. As we shall see shortly, a variety of problems arise in connection with legal norms' logical form, challenging the idea that legal norms are partial grounds of legal facts (M1–2), or of grounding facts (M2–M3), or that they function as some other kind of explanantia (M4). And some powerful objections that start with premises concerning the temporal and modal profile of

---

[44] I will point out when positivism and nonpositivism would plausibly disagree on the content of the legal norm under discussion, and will highlight how, if at all, that affects the dialectic.

legal facts and norms can be levelled against M1–4. Ultimately, these problems will cast doubt on norms' explanatory role, thereby supporting a broadly Humean view of legal norms, according to which they are explanatorily inert generalizations that do not govern the instantiation of the legal properties they are about, but rather merely summarize them.[45]

3.1 Explanatory Norms

We begin with models that invoke laws as partial explanantia of legal facts. Consider again the fact that Esther has the right to vote in US elections. If asked why that is the case, in most contexts it would suffice to point out that she has the appropriate age and citizenship to be able to vote. Yet, crucially, the fact that this response would be felicitous in many contexts is compatible with thinking that the explanation thereby given is no more than a convenient shorthand. If someone wanted the whole story, one may think, we should mention not only Esther's age and citizenship but also the fact that it is the law in the US that eighteen-year-old US citizens have the right to vote in elections. Legal norms, in this view, are crucial – if often tacit – ingredients in legal explanations (see Enoch 2011, 2019; Rosen 2017a, 2017b).

After all, it seems obvious that particular legal facts counterfactually depend on legal norms: if the norms had been suitably different, different legal facts would have obtained. If, say, the law had been that only citizens who are at least twenty-one years old have the right to vote, then eighteen-year-old Esther would not have had that right. And although counterfactual dependence is not the same as metaphysical dependence,[46] it does suggest the presence of an underlying relation of dependence that would explain it.[47] Just as the fact that changing one's age can make a difference to whether one can vote is due to the fact that one's age *explains* whether one can vote, the fact that changing the voting laws can make a difference to whether one can vote might be similarly due to the fact that the laws also help to explain this.

The view that norms feature in explanations is also reflected in the role that we routinely assign to them in legal reasoning. When a lawyer wants to know what legal features a particular has, they usually look for two elements: the facts of the case and the laws that apply to them. Only then can they establish the conclusion, which they reach by performing an inference from the facts *and* the

---

[45] A similarly Humean conception is endorsed by Epstein (2015) for social rules and by Berker (2019) for moral principles. A metaphysical model for explaining legal facts that is based on a Humean conception of legal norms will be developed in Section 3.8, under the heading "Model 5."
[46] To use Fine's famous example again, [Socrates exists] counterfactually depends on [{Socrates} exists], yet fails to metaphysically depend on it.
[47] See Schaffer (2016) for an elaboration of this point.

laws. A straightforward explanation of this aspect of legal epistemology is that laws are essential premises in arguments for conclusions about legal particulars because facts about legal particulars are metaphysically explained by laws.

In short, what motivates the idea that legal norms must be part of the explanation of legal facts is that without them, legal explanations look objectionably incomplete, both modally and epistemically. Let us call this the motivation from *norms' apparent role in explanation*. I take it that it is a desideratum for any view of the matter that it should make good on this idea, or at least find a convincing way of explaining it away. Yet, crucially, there are different ways of trying to satisfy this desideratum and, as we shall see, none of them is immune from problems.

3.2 Legal Norms as Partial Grounds: Models 1–2

A clear way of vindicating the role of legal norms in explanation is to posit them as additional partial grounds of legal facts. Since any ground is an explanans of what it grounds, the appearance that legal norms are explanatory is obviously vindicated by assigning this role to them. On this model, let us call it Model 1 (M1), each particular legal fact is grounded in two sorts of ingredients (see Figure 1): (i) some legal norm(s) connecting the legal property (or relation) involved in the target legal fact to some underlying properties (or relations), and (ii) some base facts involving the instantiation of the properties (or relations) singled out by the correlative legal norm.[48]

A short but compelling argument appears to provide substantial support in favor of M1. Suppose, for *reductio*, that [Esther has the right to vote in US elections] is fully grounded in [Esther is an eighteen-year-old US citizen]. By GROUNDING NECESSITARIANISM,[49] it follows that every world where Esther is an eighteen-year-old US citizen is a world where she has the right to vote in US elections. But that seems false. For surely the law that sets out voting

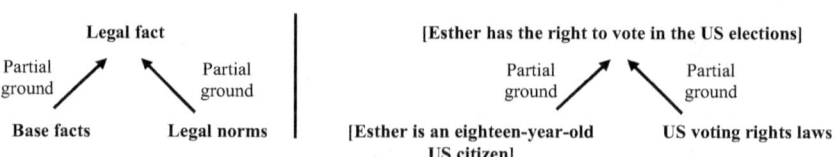

Figure 1 Model 1: General and applied to a case.

---

[48] This model is endorsed by Enoch (2019) and Rosen (2017a, 2017b). It is also advocated by Schaffer (2019) in connection with particular social facts.
[49] Remember that GROUNDING NECESSITARIANISM says that grounds metaphysically necessitate what they ground: if at the actual world some facts Γ fully ground [*p*], then it's absolutely impossible for all the facts in Γ to obtain without [*p*] obtaining as well.

requirements is metaphysically contingent, and so there are worlds with different laws where Esther is an eighteen-year-old US citizen but doesn't have the right to vote. If so, then [Esther is an eighteen-year-old US citizen] is at best a mere partial ground of [Esther has the right to vote in US elections], from which it follows that something needs to be added to ground the latter fact. And the legal norms connecting the target legal properties with the underlying conditions seem ideally placed to fill this gap. For not only is it intuitive that legal norms are part of the reason why legal facts obtain, but adding them to the grounding base is also the key to preserving GROUNDING NECESSITARIANISM: every world where Esther is an eighteen-year-old US citizen *and* where it is the law that eighteen-year-old citizens have the right to vote *is* a world where Esther has the right to vote. In Section 3.8, we will see how this line of argument might be resisted (besides merely rejecting GROUNDING NECESSITARIANISM). For now, it suffices to note that it provides a powerful reason in favor of taking legal norms as partial grounds of legal facts.

An interesting extension of Model 1 may be provided to account for an additional explanatory role that legal norms might be thought to play. It may seem plausible that legal norms explain not only legal facts but also the fact that legal facts depend on the base facts that they do. You may ask: why is having a certain age and citizenship the fact in virtue of which one has the voting rights that one does? Because the law says so, the answer goes.

As before, this is reflected in the existence of a counterfactual connection, this time holding between the fact about the *grounding connection* linking legal facts and base facts on the one hand, and the relevant legal norm on the other. Not only would the fact that one has the right to vote fail to obtain if the relevant legal norms were different; the fact that one's right to vote depends on one's age and citizenship would also fail to obtain. Therefore one might suppose that legal norms also explain why legal facts are grounded in the base facts that they are. If we again treat this kind of explanation as a grounding explanation, then this leads to an extension of Model 1 that conjoins it with the claim that the fact that a legal fact is grounded in the base facts that it is is, in turn, grounded in the relevant legal norm(s). On this model – let us call it Model 2 (M2) – legal norms play two explanatory roles (see Figure 2): they ground both (i) the target legal facts and (ii) the grounding connection between them and the base facts that ground them.

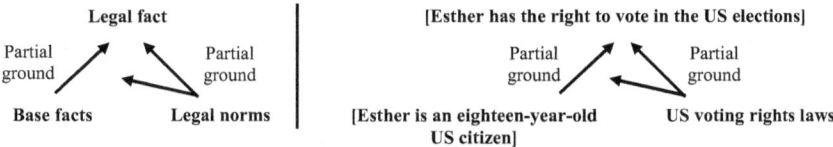

Figure 2 Model 2: General and applied to a case.

Notice that the grounding relation that holds between legal norms and the grounding facts in question should be regarded as a relation of partial grounding. For the existence of a legal norm is clearly compatible with the absence of the legal fact and the base fact whose grounding connection it actually grounds. So given the factivity of ground, the existence of the legal norm is compatible with the absence of the grounding fact that it actually grounds.

As an example, consider again the norm that eighteen-year-old US citizens can vote in elections. At the world-time pair $\{@, t\}$, Esther is an eighteen-year-old US citizen, and the voting law grounds [[Esther is an eighteen-year-old US citizen] grounds [Esther has the right to vote]]. Yet Esther could have failed to be a US citizen (if, say, she had been born outside the US to noncitizen parents, and was never naturalized), in which case she wouldn't have had the right to vote in the US (keeping the voting laws fixed). So it is possible for the actual voting laws to exist without it being the case that Esther's being an eighteen-year-old US citizen grounds her having the right to vote. So again, assuming GROUNDING NECESSITARIANISM, the voting law cannot be a full ground for [[Esther is an eighteen-year-old US citizen] grounds [Esther has the right to vote]].

This naturally raises the question of what should be added to complete the explanation of this grounding fact. On a conservative account, appealing also to [Esther is an eighteen-year-old US citizen] as an additional ground may be thought to provide an adequate basis. For worlds where the norm that eighteen-year-old US citizens have the right to vote exists *and* where Esther is an eighteen-year-old US citizen *are* worlds where [Esther is an eighteen-year-old US citizen] grounds [Esther has the right to vote]. Thus the legal norms, combined with the satisfaction of their "antecedent" conditions, necessitate both the target legal facts and the grounding connection between them and their base facts. Perhaps there are better ways of completing Model 2, but we won't pursue this matter further. The key element of M2 that interests us here is simply that legal norms play this double role of first-order grounds and meta-grounds.[50]

3.3 Problems of Logical Form

What form, then, do legal norms have? When, in the preceding sections, we gave a rough gloss of the law that putatively figures in explanations of facts about people's right to vote, we described it as the norm that *US citizens who are at least eighteen years old have the right to vote in general elections*. Taking this

---

[50] Alternative, more complex views may involve additional elements, such as facts about the essence of some of the items contained in the grounding facts, but we shall set those views aside for the time being.

The Metaphysics of Legal Facts

surface form as a faithful guide to logical form leads to viewing legal norms as having the form of generalizations:

[GEN] $\forall x \, (\varphi(x) \rightarrow Fx)$

with the specific norm in question taking the form:

[GEN-V] $\forall x \, ((x$ is at least eighteen years old $\wedge \ x$ is a US citizen$) \rightarrow x$ has the right to vote in US elections)

This proposal, however, is deeply problematic (see Rosen 2017a: 287). For accidental generalizations – that is, facts with the form of unprefixed universally quantified claims – are plausibly grounded in their instances,[51] which in this case are facts about material conditionals of the form $[\varphi(a) \rightarrow Fa]$.[52] And conditional facts with true consequents are plausibly grounded in their consequents, $[Fa]$, just as disjunctions are grounded in their true disjuncts.[53] Yet on the models we are considering (M1 and M2), legal norms are taken to be *grounds* of such facts, and so construing them as generalizations leads to violating the asymmetry (and, via transitivity, the irreflexivity) of grounding (see Figure 3).

A natural response might be to construe legal norms as *prefixed* generalizations, that is, as general facts involving some kind of intensional or hyperintensional operator, such as 'according to the law of s,' along the following lines:

[Law] According to the law of s, p.

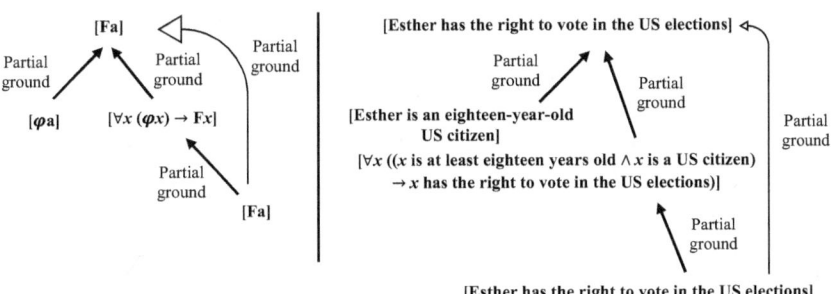

Figure 3 Violations of asymmetry and irreflexivity.

---

[51] For example, $[\forall x \, Fx]$ is plausibly grounded in $[Fa]$, $[Fb]$, ….. See, e.g., Fine (2012: 59), Rosen (2017b: 142), and Skiles (2015: §4).

[52] In this case, [Gen-V] is plausibly grounded in [(Esther is at least eighteen years old $\wedge$ Esther is a US citizen) $\rightarrow$ Esther has the right to vote in US elections], and so on for each actually obtaining instance.

[53] For instance, the fact that Esther has the right to vote in US elections (see Rosen 2017b: 142).

If laws are understood in this way, then this problem should not arise. First, prefixed facts of this kind, like modalized facts more generally, are plausibly not grounded in their instances (Rosen 2010).[54] Second, in the legal case specifically, it is especially implausible to think that facts of the form of [Law] might be grounded in this way. As Rosen (2017b: 143) usefully remarks: "Despite the wide diversity of views, no one thinks that what makes it the case that it's illegal to drive down Main Street at 80 mph is the fact that particular token acts of speeding down Main Street, past, present, and future, happen to be illegal."

In addition to this, the view that laws' internal structure has this form comports well with the pretheoretical observation that when we routinely make claims about the content of valid legal norms, we do so in various more or less interchangeable ways that involve the use of such operators: 'according to the law of system s, p,' 'under the law of s, p,' 'it is the law in s that p,' 'the norm that p is legally valid in s,' and the like. Further, the fact that legal norms should be viewed as prefixed, rather than naked, generalizations is also independently clear from the fact that when we appeal to them in legal explanations, we appeal to what the law says, and no law is law *simpliciter*, but rather only relative to a particular system.[55]

Construing the general facts that supposedly ground legal facts in this way, however, only tells us this much about the form of laws. In particular, it doesn't tell us anything about the *internal structure* of the prefixed content that norms have.[56] And, broadly speaking, two paths ahead seem to be the most promising at this point. The first elaborates on the refinements above and regards laws as mere prefixed *generalizations*, while the second views them as endowed not only with an explanatory role but also with *explanatory content*.

3.4 Explanatory Norms with Nonexplanatory Content

If we conservatively apply the revisions outlined earlier, we get a conception of laws' structure as prefixed universally quantified conditionals or biconditionals, derived from the addition of the prefix to [Gen], as in:

[Gen-Law] According to the law of s, $\forall x \, (\varphi(x) \to Fx)$.[57]

---

[54] For instance, on the view advocated by Fine (1994) and Rosen (2010), facts about necessity and possibility are grounded in facts about essence.

[55] We say that Esther has the right to vote because it is *the law in the US* that eighteen-year-old citizens have the right to vote, not because, generically, eighteen-year-old citizens have that right.

[56] For the sake of simplicity, I'm assuming that all legal norms have a general form, but all I say here – both the problems and the solutions I outline – can be rephrased, *mutatis mutandis*, for norms with a particular form, if such there be.

[57] Or as in:

[Gen-Law'] According to the law of s, $\forall x \, (\varphi x) \leftrightarrow Fx)$.

On this elaboration of models M1–2, legal facts of the form [Fa] are always fully grounded in general norms of the form [GEN-LAW] together with base facts of the form [$\varphi(a)$]. For instance, [Esther has the right to vote in US elections] will be grounded in [According to US law, all eighteen-year-old US citizens have the right to vote in US elections] together with [Esther is an eighteen-year-old US citizen].

This sort of account, however, faces a serious problem, highlighted by Rosen (2017a: 293). The problem is that if the operator 'according to the law (of s)' is closed under logical consequence, then it will threaten to generate countless bogus explanations. For instance, given closure and antecedent strengthening, from

[GEN-LAW-V] According to the law of s, $\forall x$ ((x is at least eighteen years old $\wedge$ x is a US citizen) $\rightarrow$ x has the right to vote in US elections).

it will follow that

[GEN-LAW-V*] According to the law of s, $\forall x$ ((x is at least eighteen years old $\wedge$ x is a US citizen $\wedge$ x is wealthy) $\rightarrow$ x has the right to vote in US elections).

And while this also has the form of [GEN-LAW], it is plausible that neither it nor facts about the satisfaction of its antecedent are grounds for particular legal facts concerning voting rights. First, Esther's being wealthy plays no role in grounding her right to vote, even if she is in fact wealthy, since any ground must be relevant to the explanation of what it grounds,[58] and Esther's being wealthy is irrelevant to her having the right to vote. Second, even if one takes it to be true that, according to US law, wealthy US citizens of age have the right to vote, it is doubtful that this fact would be responsible for explaining anyone's right to vote. For, again, it seems irrelevant to Esther's (or anyone else's) right to vote that under US law, *wealthy* US citizens have the right to vote in elections.

One solution to this problem might be to drop closure and deny that, in general, the logical consequences of what the law says are law.[59] This would then allow one to say, for instance, that it does not follow from its being the law in the US that eighteen-year-old US citizens can vote that it is the law in the US that wealthy eighteen-year-old US citizens can vote, and to thereby deny that this latter fact obtains.

---

[58] This, remember, is what is often taken to justify the assumption that grounding, unlike supervenience and necessitation, is nonmonotonic.

[59] Alternatively, one could keep closure and employ a nonclassical relevance logic to disallow the irrelevant implications of legal norms to count as norms. This option is pursued in Moreso (1996).

This strategy, however, may sound too drastic: after all, wealthy US citizens *do* have the right to vote under US law, even though no particular citizen has that right in virtue of being wealthy. What should be opposed, in other words, is not that the law says this (i.e., that [Gen-Law-V*] obtains), but rather that this law, or facts about the instantiation of its conditions, participate in the explanation of particular legal facts.

This last observation motivates a different solution that preserves closure but discriminates, among facts of the form [Gen-Law], between those that do and those that do not play an explanatory role. The starting point is that even if closure holds, M1–2 are *not* committed to regarding facts such as [Gen-Law-V*], or facts about the satisfaction of their antecedents, as grounds for legal facts. These models say that every legal fact is grounded in a combination of base facts together with legal norms of the form given by [Gen-Law], but they do *not* say that every fact of the form [Gen-Law] is a ground of a particular legal fact. So it is open to the advocate of M1–2 to think of the form of legal norms along the lines of [Gen-Law], and keep closure (thereby allowing for facts such as [Gen-Law-V*]), while denying that legal facts are grounded in facts such as [Gen-Law-V*].

To emphasize: the view we are considering denies that whenever facts of the form [According to the law of s, $\forall x\ (\varphi(x) \rightarrow Fx)$] and [$\varphi(a)$] obtain, they will ground a fact of the form [Fa]. For, given a genuine law with that form, closure generates countless facts that share the same form but play no role in grounding [Fa]. Yet, crucially, this is compatible with endorsing M1–2. For these views merely hold that each legal fact of the form [Fa] must be grounded in *some* plurality of facts of the form [According to the law of s, $\forall x\ (\varphi(x) \rightarrow Fx)$], [$\varphi(a)$]. If one wishes to reserve the label "legal norm" or "law" just for facts that do play this grounding role, then the current reply strategy can be expressed by saying that not all facts of the form [According to the law of s, $\forall x\ (\varphi(x) \rightarrow Fx)$] correspond to genuine laws or legal norms.

Although this seems a viable solution, it does raise a difficult question. If not all facts of the form [Gen-Law] are genuine laws, then logical form alone won't allow us to distinguish real laws from bogus ones (Rosen 2017a: 293). This poses the challenge of providing a criterion for distinguishing, among facts of the form [According to the law of s, $\forall x\ (\varphi(x) \rightarrow Fx)$], between those that do and those that do not play a role in grounding explanations of legal facts – between those that do and those that do not express genuine laws. It is an open question whether this challenge can ultimately be met.[60]

---

[60] Rosen (2017b) takes up this challenge in connection with moral laws and explanations (where the same problem arises), but it remains to be seen both whether that strategy works and, if it does, whether an analogous solution could be fashioned for the case of legal norms.

3.5 Explanatory Norms with Explanatory Content

A different sort of strategy to deal with the problem of bogus laws seeks to block the problematic result by exploring the hypothesis that on top of playing an explanatory role, laws also have explanatory content. The problem was that facts of the form of [GEN-LAW], which merely establish sufficient conditions for the instantiation of the target legal property or relation, are not necessarily explanatory. So one possible way out could be to modify one's conception of legal norms' internal structure to prevent the generation of pseudo-laws via closure.

One promising way of doing this, pursued by Rosen (2017a), is to conceive of legal norms as having explanatory content. The rough idea is that when a law connects the instantiation of a legal property F to the satisfaction of some underlying conditions φ, it does not merely say that anything that is φ is also F. Rather, it says that anything that is φ is *thereby* F, that is, that φ-things are F *because* they are φ (Rosen 2017a: 293–4):

[Ex-Law] According to the law of s, $\forall x \, (\varphi(x) \rightarrow [\varphi(x)]$ explains $[Fx])$.

Armed with this conception of laws, M1–2 could maintain that legal facts of the form [Fa] are always fully grounded in some base fact [$\varphi(a)$] together with a law to the effect that anything that is φ is such that its being φ explains its being F. Notice how this solves the earlier problem (Rosen 2017a: 294). To work with the specific case we've been using, the relevant norm would be:

[Ex-Law-V] According to the law of s, $\forall x$ ((x is at least eighteen years old ∧ x is a US citizen) → [x is at least eighteen years old ∧ x is a US citizen] explains [x has the right to vote in US elections]).

And from this, it won't follow that

[Ex-Law-V*] According to the law of s, $\forall x$ ((x is at least eighteen years old ∧ x is a US citizen ∧ x is wealthy) → [x is at least eighteen years old ∧ x is a US citizen ∧ x is wealthy] explains [x has the right to vote in US elections]).

For [Ex-Law-V*] involves not merely a strengthening of the antecedent but also a modification of the consequent. Notice, further, that while [Ex-Law-V] does classically entail

[Ex-Law-V'] According to the law of s, $\forall x$ ((x is at least eighteen years old ∧ x is a US citizen ∧ x is wealthy) → [x is at least eighteen years old ∧ x is a US citizen] explains [x has the right to vote in US elections]).

this is not a problem (Rosen 2017a: 295). For one thing is for it to be the case that under US law, wealthy US citizens of age have the right to vote *because they are US citizens of age*, and another, quite different thing is for it to be the case that according to US law, wealthy US citizens of age have the right to vote *because they are wealthy US citizens of age*. The former norm follows from the fact that under US law, US citizens of age have the right to vote because they are US citizens of age, but it is unproblematic. And the latter would be problematic, but it doesn't follow from that fact.

Rosen's proposal solves the problem of bogus laws while retaining closure, but it raises the question of what kind of explanation figures in the laws thus conceived. Since we've seen that neither causation nor modal relations capture the relation between legal facts and base facts, it is implausible that either would give us the notion we need.

One possibility mentioned by Rosen (2017a: 296), is to take this to be a *generic* form of explanation. The hope would be to find some core notion of explanation that is shared by all explanatory relations (grounding, causation, etc.), and which could be used for the purpose in question. Specifically, the idea would be that grounding, causation, and other relations belong to the class of explanatory relations in virtue of pertaining to a common genus of which they are species, and in terms of which they are to be defined. If this is true, then there might be an interesting, general notion of explanation in the background that could figure in the content of laws.

That said, as things stand, it is fair to say that the prospects of this strategy look uncertain. For one thing, it is far from clear that such a generic notion of explanation exists. In particular, granting that grounding, causation, and so on all belong to a common class of explanation, it is unclear what the relationship between them and that class is. Perhaps there is nothing significant that these relations share, and they are mere determinates of a determinable notion of explanation with no interesting set of common features. Furthermore, even if an interesting common *genus* does exist, it is unclear what it would be like, and whether it could be used for the specific task of filling in [Ex-Law]. So although this may be a research path worth pursuing, it is safer to explore some alternative responses.

An obvious suggestion would be to take 'explain' in [Ex-Law] to mean *metaphysically grounds*, yielding laws with the following structure:

[G-Law] According to the law of s, $\forall x\ (\varphi(x) \to [\varphi(x)]$ metaphysically grounds $[Fx])$.

This immediately raises the question of whether the notion of grounding invoked by the law is that of full or partial ground. Precisifying [G-Law] as involving a relation of full grounding will give us:

[FG-Law] According to the law of s, $\forall x\ (\varphi(x) \rightarrow [\varphi(x)]$ fully metaphysically grounds [Fx]).

Now, this formulation of legal norms need not be objectionable in itself.[61] What is objectionable, however, is to combine it with M1 or M2. For if the actual norms have the form of [FG-Law], then it seems to follow that base facts are full grounds of the legal facts they ground.[62] Yet according to M1–2, base facts are mere partial grounds. So norms that take the form [FG-Law] contradict M1–2 (see also Epstein 2015).[63] Relatedly, while, strictly speaking, legal norms' having this form does not rule out their being additional partial grounds of legal facts, they could only play this role by overdetermining them. Yet the spirit of M1–2 is that legal norms should play a significant role in legal explanations, and the redundant role they'd be left with violates this spirit. So it seems that legal norms cannot both have this explanatory content and also play an explanatory role (compare with Berker 2019).[64]

An alternative proposal would be to take legal norms to make a claim of partial grounding:[65]

---

[61] We'll come back to its possible shortcomings when dealing with Model 5, which relies on it.

[62] This step may be challenged, if the operator 'according to the law' isn't factive. Nonfactivity would allow [FG-Law] to be combined with the view that legal norms are nonredundant partial grounds, i.e., with M1-2. This solution may be of special interest given that there seem to be independent reasons to think that the law can state falsehoods, with legal fictions providing a clear case of this phenomenon.

[63] Epstein (2015: 121) makes this point in connection with the explanation of particular social facts. He points out that if social rules involve a relation of full ground between target social properties and the underlying socially relevant properties, then such rules cannot play a role in grounding particular social facts. He then goes on to make the stronger claim that since it is plausible that social rules do have this structure, this gives us a good reason to reject "conjunctivism," which is the analogue of Model 1 for social facts. Conjunctivism, in our jargon, holds that particular social facts are partly grounded in social rules and partly grounded in base facts.

[64] Berker (2019: 911) makes this argument in the moral case, which he calls the 'Problem of Redundant Grounding.' Berker (2019: 909) labels as 'Principles as Partial Grounds' the view that particular moral facts are fully grounded in a combination of moral principles connecting certain moral properties with underlying properties, together with facts concerning the instantiation of the latter. (This is the moral analogue of Model 1.) Then he maintains that moral principles plausibly have explanatory full-grounding content, analogously to [FG-Law]. From this, he argues that moral principles can only be redundant grounds of particular moral facts, and concludes that since this is implausible, Principles as Partial Grounds should be rejected. Berker (2019: 913–16) and Epstein (2015: 121–3) discuss and reject various attempts to rescue full-grounding norms in the cases of moral principles and social rules respectively.

[65] This parallels one of the accounts that Schaffer (2019: 761–2) proposes for the content of social rules.

[PG-Law] According to the law of s, $\forall x \, (\varphi(x) \rightarrow [\varphi(x)]$ partially metaphysically grounds [Fx]).

Unlike the previous proposal, this formulation fits well with the view, expressed by M1–2, that base facts are partial grounds of legal facts. Because of this, it also allows for the possibility that legal norms themselves play a nonredundant grounding role, thereby enabling a faithful implementation of these models. Are there any reasons to resist it?[66]

One possible worry is that this conception of the form of legal norms sits uncomfortably with the role that they are meant to play. The function of a legal norm is to regulate or constitute a certain property or relation, to tell us what needs to be the case in order for someone or something to instantiate it. Legal norms address questions ("Under what conditions is one a citizen?," "What is legally prohibited?") and give us guidance by providing authoritative answers to them. But how could they fulfill this role, unless they specified the full grounds of the property or relation in question? To leave out part of the explanation might seem objectionably incomplete.[67]

If legal norms are meant to specify the complete set of conditions that lead to the instantiation of the legal property they regulate, yet they cannot make a claim of full metaphysical ground, then a possible solution may come from appealing to a sort of grounding pluralism, that is, to the idea that there's a plurality of grounding relations. In a moderate form, grounding pluralism has been advocated by Fine (2012), who has argued that there are three fundamentally distinct notions of grounding: metaphysical, natural, and normative grounding, exemplified by claims such as the following (Fine 2012: 37):

METAPHYSICAL   The fact that the ball is red and round obtains in virtue of the fact that it is red and the fact that it is round.

NATURAL   The fact that the particle is accelerating obtains in virtue of the fact that it is being acted upon by some net positive force.

NORMATIVE   The fact that their action is wrong obtains in virtue of the fact that it was done with the sole intention of causing harm.

These three kinds of grounding are fundamentally distinct, according to Fine, in the sense that none of them is reducible to any of the others, or definable in terms of a common generic notion. Further, each of them is related to its own primitive

---

[66] Berker (2019) and Enoch (2019) reject the analogue of [PG-Law] for moral principles.

[67] DeRosset (2025) raises this worry for legal norms. To solve this problem, he develops a self-referential view of legal norms on which they provide full grounds by mentioning themselves. Berker (2019) and Rosen (2017a) express skepticism about this strategy.

modality: metaphysical grounds metaphysically necessitate what they ground, natural grounds naturally necessitate what they ground, and normative grounds normatively necessitate what they ground.

In this spirit, Enoch (2019) proposes that we should also countenance a relation of *legal* grounding. Legal grounding is meant to be the explanatory relation that holds within the framework set up by the law. Within the legal story, as it were, the fact that Esther is an eighteen-year-old US citizen fully explains why she has the right to vote in US elections. More generally, legal norms create a narrative within which base facts are the full legal grounds of particular legal facts, and nothing else is needed to explain them. Interestingly, moreover, notice that this being so is compatible with holding that in the global metaphysical hierarchy, the full explanation of legal facts will involve both the underlying base facts *and* the legal norms themselves.

Insofar as one is happy to countenance a plurality of grounding relations, the notion of legal grounding – of "grounding within the law" – may be used to characterize legal norms in the obvious way:

[LG-Law] According to the law of s, $\forall x\, (\varphi(x) \to [\varphi(x)]$ legally grounds $[Fx])$.

Now, the key question is whether this notion of legal grounding is definable in terms of a more basic grounding relation or is rather primitive. Taking it as primitive may seem objectionable, for it would threaten to give us a recipe for the proliferation of primitive grounding relations across the board. Within the game of chess, checkmating one's opponent grounds winning the game. So checkmating chessly grounds winning a game of chess. Within the rules of English, spelling the first-person pronoun with a lower-case "i" makes it the case that one made a grammatical mistake. So writing "i" to refer to oneself orthographically grounds misspelling the word. And so on. This seems clearly absurd (see Rosen 2017a: 286; although see Enoch 2019 for an attempt to vindicate this strategy).

On the other hand, if legal grounding is not primitive, then the obvious way of defining it would be in terms of metaphysical grounding and legal norms, along the following lines:

LEGAL GROUNDING For a particular legal fact of the form $[Fa]$ to be legally grounded in some underlying conditions $[\varphi(a)]$ is for $[Fa]$ to be metaphysically grounded in $[\varphi(a)]$ together with [LG-Law].

That is, to be legally grounded in some fact is to be metaphysically grounded in it, together with the relevant norm. Legal grounds are just metaphysical grounds that combine with laws.

The main problem with this proposal, as noticed by Rosen (2017b: 156) in the parallel moral case, is that this definition is circular. For the definiens of the legal grounding relation involves [LG-Law], which in turn involves the definiendum, that is, the very notion of legal grounding that it seeks to define. Since it is unclear how else the notion of legal grounding may be defined, it is unclear how promising it would be to rely on this idea.

3.6 Legal Norms as Meta-Grounds and Linking Principles: Models 3–4

The only account of legal norms' logical form, among those considered here, that was apparently exempt from problems is [FG-Law]. On this account, legal norms relate target legal properties with some underlying conditions by stating that facts about the former are fully metaphysically grounded in facts about the latter. The problem arising in connection with this account did not concern the account per se, but rather the untenability of combining it with M1 or M2. According to M1–2, legal norms are partial grounds of legal facts; and yet how can this be true, if legal norms' content is that base facts on their own fully ground legal facts? This suggests that perhaps the best response to the challenges we've met is to reject these models.

Now, one may think that if we accept [FG-Law] as the correct account of norms' logical form, and reject M1–2, then we're necessarily left with a Humean conception of legal norms that rejects their apparent role in explanations.[68] But this would be a mistake, since [FG-Law] is compatible with views that do assign an explanatory role to laws, if only a role that is different from that of being partial grounds of particular legal facts.

One such view – let us call it Model 3 (M3) – can be extracted from M2 by dropping the claim that legal norms are partial metaphysical grounds of legal facts. Then, M3 is the view that whenever some particular legal fact is (fully) grounded in some base facts, a connecting norm grounds this grounding fact. This model vindicates at least one sense in which norms are often held to be explanatory, as we've seen. Why is the right to vote explained by one's age and citizenship, one may ask? Because there is a law that regulates voting rights, which establishes that anyone with a certain age and citizenship (thereby) has the right to vote (see Figure 4).

---

[68] 'Humean' here is used to indicate that just as Humean laws of nature play no explanatory role, on this conception the same is true of legal norms: both are mere summaries of patterns, and don't explain their instances. Still, a potential disanalogy is that, unlike Humean natural laws, Humean legal norms would summarize patterns of grounding relations, if they were understood as having the form [FG-Law]. Moreover, legal norms, even on a Humean conception, are plausibly not explained by their instances.

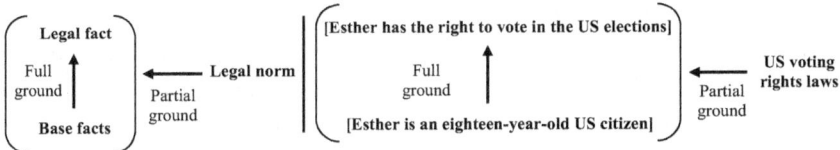

Figure 4 Model 3: In general and applied to a case.

Two clarifications are in order. First, M3 takes legal norms to ground facts about grounding. But are they full or partial grounds? For reasons discussed earlier (see Section 3.2), to regard them as full grounds would violate GROUNDING NECESSITARIANISM. So they must be partial grounds. What, then, are their partners in ground? As we saw in Section 3.2, one option would be for legal norms to ground grounding facts in combination with base facts. But this is strictly optional to M3, and there may be better options.

Second, while M3 may in principle be combined with a number of different views regarding the form of the relevant laws (including [GEN-LAW]), given the problems we've discussed, the most natural proposal is to couple it with [FG-LAW]. We then get the result that, according to this version of M3, (i) every particular legal fact of the form [Fa] is fully grounded in some base facts of the form [$\varphi(a)$]; and (ii) whenever [$\varphi(a)$] fully grounds [Fa], this fact is in turn fully grounded in a fact of the form [According to the law of s, $\forall x\,(\varphi(x) \to [\varphi(x)]$ fully metaphysically grounds [Fx])], together with [$\varphi(a)$].

There are two main difficulties with M3, one for each of the claims it makes.[69] The first is that it holds that legal facts are fully grounded in base facts and, as we've seen, this seems to lead to an absurd conclusion via GROUNDING NECESSITARIANISM. Since this problem is shared by all the models we'll consider from now on – as they all take base facts to be full grounds – we shall deal with this at the end.

The second difficulty, which affects M3 specifically, concerns its second claim. Model 3 makes a claim about the grounds of a kind of grounding fact: it holds that whenever some base facts ground a legal fact, this fact is grounded in some legal norms (possibly together with facts about the fulfillment of underlying conditions). Now, this claim may or may not be true, but it is worth highlighting that it clashes with the main views on the question of what grounds facts about grounding.

Three main answers to this question have been offered in the literature. On the "collapse" view advocated by Bennett (2011) and deRosset (2013), facts of the form [Γ fully grounds [p]] are always fully grounded in Γ. On the essentialist

---

[69] Other possible problems for the moral analogue of M3 are presented by Berker (2019).

view held by Dasgupta (2014a), Fine (2012), and Rosen (2010, 2017a), whenever Γ grounds [p], there is always some item or items $x_1 \ldots x_n$ drawn from Γ or [p] such that it lies in their nature that whenever the facts Γ obtain, they ground the fact that p. On this basis, the account then says that [Γ fully grounds [p]] is grounded in Γ, together with this fact about the essence of $x_1 \ldots x_n$. Finally, on the zero-grounding view put forward by Litland (2017), all grounding facts are zero-grounded, that is, grounded in the empty set. Since M3 is incompatible with any of these views, there are reasons to doubt its truth.

This takes us to our last hypothesis concerning the explanatory role of laws. So far, we've been assuming that if legal norms play an explanatory role, they do so by grounding some thing or another, in one way or another. This, however, leaves out one important option that we haven't considered thus far. On a unionist conception of grounding, grounding is identical to metaphysical explanation. To say that Γ metaphysically explains [p] is just to say that Γ grounds [p], and vice versa. Thus, on this conception, each explanans of a grounded fact must be one of its grounds, and grounding explanations have only two parts: what is grounded and what grounds it. Accordingly, within this conception the only explanatory role left for legal norms is that of being partial grounds.

However, as we saw in Section 2.3.1, this is not the only available conception of grounding. On a competing separatist view, grounding backs metaphysical explanation without being identical to it, and although every ground is an explanans of what it grounds, the converse need not be true. In particular, on one way of developing separatism (see Schaffer 2016, 2017a, 2017b), grounding explanations are built from three irreducible elements: grounds, grounded, and grounding principles connecting them. This way of modeling metaphysical explanation is conceived by its proponents as just a particular instantiation of the structure of explanation more generally. Explanation is thought of as having a tripartite structure that always involves sources, links, and results: sources generate results via linking principles (Schaffer 2016, 2017a). Sources on their own generate nothing, since links are also needed in order to produce them. And to regard links as additional sources would be to commit a category mistake.

This general structure is realized by different types of explanation in similar ways. In causal explanation, there are causes (e.g., the rock striking the window), laws (laws of nature), and effects (e.g., the shattering of the window). No effect follows from its causes absent a suitable law of nature; and to regard laws as causes would be a category mistake. In logical explanation, there are premises, inference rules, and conclusions. No conclusion follows from its premises absent a suitable inference rule; and to regard inference rules as premises would be to commit a category mistake. In metaphysical explanation, there are grounds, groundeds, and grounding principles, which Schaffer (2016, 2017a, 2017b) calls "laws of metaphysics." No derivative entity can arise from its grounds absent a grounding principle connecting them. And to regard grounding principles as further grounds would again be a mistake.

To take a simple example, the existence of a singleton – say, {Socrates} – can only be generated from the existence of its member, Socrates, together with the operation of set formation. Given Socrates as its input, set formation delivers {Socrates} as the output. To take another example, one might think that moral facts can only be generated from nonmoral facts in combination with some moral law connecting moral properties with nonmoral properties. In the same vein, legal norms would function as grounding principles that connect target legal properties with underlying conditions, and give rise to legal facts in combination with facts about the satisfaction of those conditions. No legal fact may be produced merely on the basis of the underlying base facts: legal norms are also needed. Yet one shouldn't conflate these norms with grounds, since they play a fundamentally different role. The resulting model – let us call it Model 4 (M4) – can be represented in the following way (see Figure 5).

According to M4, legal facts are fully metaphysically grounded in base facts, but are also metaphysically explained by legal norms, without being grounded in them. Legal norms are explanantia, but not grounds.

This model raises a number of difficult questions regarding what form legal norms, conceived as grounding principles, should have, as well as whether they are suitable to play this role. It is an open and interesting question, for instance, whether [FG-Law] would be the right form for legal grounding laws to have. It certainly speaks in its favor that [FG-Law] can be used within M4 without undermining its key tenets, as it did with M1–2. But, apart from this, it should be noted that none of the main accounts of metaphysical laws that are currently on offer takes this form. On Schaffer's (2016) view, grounding principles are taken to be dependence functions modeled through structural equations. On Glazier's (2016) view, they are expressed through a distinctive two-place sentential operator introduced for this particular purpose. And on Wilsch's (2016) deductive-nomological model, which follows Hempel and Oppenheim's (1948) famous account of scientific explanation, they take the form of quantified conditionals.

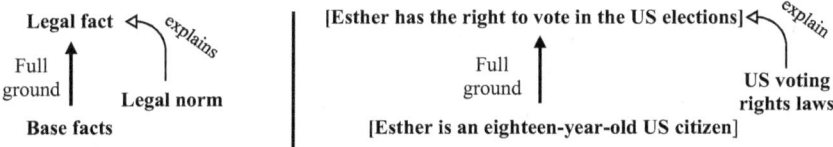

Figure 5 Model 4: In general and applied to a case.

Another source of skepticism is that metaphysical laws are usually taken to be metaphysically necessary, whereas legal norms are clearly not. Relatedly, by virtue of being a "third" element in explanations, distinct from grounds and groundeds, they are often conceived as ungrounded or not apt for being grounded, while legal norms surely cannot be fundamental and have to be grounded in some underlying facts. Correlatively, they should also be much more general in their scope of application. Going back to the case of singleton sets, there is a unique function, set formation, that takes in certain inputs and returns certain outputs. It is not as if there is one grounding principle for the construction of {Socrates}, another quite different law for the construction of {Plato}, and so on. Yet since each legal norm is different, and different laws are involved in the explanation of different legal facts, to regard them as metaphysical laws would be to do precisely this.

Therefore, if there are any metaphysical laws at work in the legal case, they would probably operate at a much higher level of abstraction, rather than the level at which specific legal norms operate. Perhaps, for instance, there could be a "law of jurisprudence" to the effect that whenever some norm is in place connecting $\varphi(x)$ and Fx, and $[\varphi(a)]$ obtains, those two things together give rise to $[Fa]$. *This* could be a metaphysical law – applying to, and thereby explaining, *all* legal facts – as in fact it might even have the modal strength of metaphysical necessity. But it would not itself be a legal norm, and in fact it would suggest that legal norms are further partial grounds of legal facts, as M1 and M2, but not M4, have it.

Perhaps this is not a knock-down objection. Perhaps, for instance, we could draw a distinction between derivative and fundamental grounding principles, treat legal norms as derivative and contingent laws, and thereby preserve a sparse basis of fundamental and necessary "laws of jurisprudence" in the face of an abundance of higher-level principles at the derivative level. But whether or not this problem can be solved is a difficult issue, and one that must be grappled with.

In this section, I have outlined four different models of how particular legal facts might be explained, and of the place of legal norms within such explanations. These models differ on the role they assign to base facts, as to whether these are partial or full grounds. They also differ on the specific explanatory role they assign to norms, as to whether these are the grounds of legal facts, the grounds of grounding facts, or grounding principles. But these models all try to accommodate the motivation we started with, that legal norms should be explanatory, and they all assume that they are explanatory. Now, we turn to a final set of objections seeking to show that the preceding models are all false.

3.7 Problems of Modal and Temporal Profile

In this section, I present a pair of structurally analogous arguments against explanatory norms. Both arguments are inspired by, and closely related to, an influential line of argument developed by Epstein (2015, 2019a, 2019b) against the view that particular social (and legal) facts are grounded in the metaphysical determinants of social (and legal) rules. However, the arguments I present do not entirely follow Epstein's, and make subtly different points (for reasons that will emerge in due course).[70] Nevertheless, they are based on the same raw material, which involves a combination of assumptions regarding the modal and temporal profile of legal facts, and structural features of grounding.

The same line of reasoning on which the arguments are based can be redirected, in slightly different ways, toward any of M1–4. However, for the sake of brevity, I will fully outline and discuss only the version that targets M1–2 specifically. Still, I will indicate how some minimal adjustments lead to rejecting the view that legal norms are partial grounds of grounding facts (as per M3), and that they are metaphysical explanantia of legal facts (as per M4). The overall conclusion is that, if these arguments are successful, some legal facts are not explained by any norms. This will then pave the way for the introduction of Model 5 (M5), which conceives of legal norms as inert generalizations.

3.7.1 The Temporal Argument Against Explanatory Norms

This variant of the temporal argument specifically targets the view, shared by M1–2, that every legal fact of the form [Fa] is partly grounded in some legal norm connecting F with an underlying condition φ, $[L(\varphi, F)]$.[71] It runs as follows:

TEMPORAL DISSONANCE   For some time t, some legal fact of the form [Fa] obtains at t and no legal norm of the form $[L(\varphi, F)]$ obtains at t.

SYNCHRONICITY Γ grounds $[p]$ only if all the facts Γ and $[p]$ obtain at the same time t.

NO GROUND$_T$ Some legal fact of the form [Fa] is not grounded in any legal norm $[L(\varphi, F)]$.

---

[70] Relatedly, Epstein focuses most of his attention on the modal version of the argument, while here I develop both variants in equal measure. While it is probably true that the modal argument is dialectically stronger than the temporal version, I think that both deserve careful scrutiny.

[71] I formulate norms in this schematic way to flag that this is meant to be neutral between the rival conceptions of their internal structure considered earlier, in Section 3.3.

Three clarifications are in order. The first premise asserts that some legal facts are temporally disjoint from any of the norms concerning the legal properties they involve as constituents. I say 'any' as opposed to 'some' for two reasons. First, because there could be more than one norm regulating the properties involved in a legal fact. Second, because we want to be neutral on the question of what form norms have, and so we need to be neutral on whether there could be a plurality of norms instantiating the form [L(φ, F)], as some of the options for legal norms' logical form canvassed earlier (Section 3.3) would have it. Either way, the argument is meant to establish that some legal facts aren't grounded in any legal norm, and therefore it should establish that legal facts aren't grounded in any legal norm of the form [L(φ, F)].

Relatedly, while the argument does not conclude that some legal facts aren't grounded in norms of any kind, this conclusion follows from the plausible added premise that if any norms are responsible for grounding legal facts, it is those connecting the properties involved in the relevant legal facts at issue (i.e., norms of the form [L(φ, F)] for facts of the form [Fa]). I omit this extra step so that we can focus on the core of the argument, but it should be implicitly understood to be there.

Third, notice that while the argument is directed against M1–2, with minor modifications it can easily be redirected against M3 and M4. As for M3, one need only substitute TEMPORAL DISSONANCE with the premise that some fact of the form [[$\varphi(a)$] fully grounds [Fa]] obtains at a time at which [L(φ, F)] does not, and it will follow, via SYNCHRONICITY, that the former fact isn't grounded in the latter. As for M4, one need only substitute SYNCHRONICITY with the principle that metaphysical explanantia and explananda (rather than grounds and groundeds) must be cotemporal, and it will follow, via TEMPORAL DISSONANCE, that [Fa] is not metaphysically explained by [L(φ, F)]. Although here we'll focus only on the argument as presented, it should become clear that these variants are equally plausible – they stand or fall together.

Let us now go back to the main argument. The motivation behind TEMPORAL DISSONANCE comes from examples. Epstein (2015) makes the point that it is not so implausible to think that social facts about the past could involve properties that are rooted, in some sense, in later practices. As Epstein (2015: 123) puts it: "We can look back at ancient societies, and evaluate whether there are classes or castes, aristocrats or serfs. We might look for baristas in the Ottoman Empire or in seventeenth-century England, and variable annuities among the ancient Egyptians."

Notice, however, that what we need here is a case of a *legal* fact obtaining prior to (or later than) the existence of the relevant legal norm. Epstein puts forward a putative case of this type, which concerns international law, and specifically the property of being a war criminal. Epstein (2015: 124) remarks: "We can sensibly ask whether Caligula was a war criminal, or whether Genghis Khan was, having killed over a million inhabitants of a single city." The idea is that even though the norms regulating war criminality, now largely collected in the Geneva Conventions of 1949, only began to exist in the late nineteenth and early twentieth centuries, we can still use them to assess whether people who committed atrocities prior to their existence qualify as war criminals. We can truly say, for instance, that since Khan ordered the slaughter of Nishapur in 1221 he was a war criminal, even though the laws of war did not exist at that time. Presumably, then, [Khan is a war criminal] obtains at 1221, even though the Geneva Conventions setting the conditions for being a war criminal start existing only in 1949. If so, then it follows by SYNCHRONICITY that [Khan is a war criminal] isn't grounded in the Conventions: some particular legal facts aren't grounded in the legal norms that regulate the legal properties they involve.

3.7.2 Replies to the Temporal Argument

The argument schema in Section 3.7.1 is valid, so the only way to block its conclusion is to reject some of its premises. One way of resisting TEMPORAL DISSONANCE would be to take issue with the cases that provide alleged instances of it. In this vein, one could have the view that the norms on war criminality are natural laws that need no positive enactment and so already existed before the Geneva Conventions formalized them, thereby regaining the cotemporality of fact and norm. This reply may be fine, as far as it goes. But the problem is that for the objection to get off the ground, it needs only one case of temporal dissonance, and this reply strategy gives us no reason to think that no such case may be found. Otherwise said: if the reader is unconvinced that the laws of war provide a case in point, they need only substitute them with another law-fact pair that exhibits the problematic schism, and it will raise the same issue. For presumably no one – not even the most extreme natural law theorist – would believe that *all* legal norms are necessary and eternal.[72]

Similarly, one could try to explain the intuitive pull of the Khan example in terms of a conflation of an ordinary and a technical legal notion of war criminality. The property of being a war criminal would be like that of being a murderer. On the ordinary notion, to be a murderer just is to kill somebody else. So people can be murderers regardless of the existence of any legal rule setting out conditions for being so. By contrast, on any of the many technical notions of murder defined by law, being a murderer does require the existence of the relevant law.

---

[72] Here I use this example for the sake of illustration and because it is the one originally proposed by Epstein (2015, 2019a, 2019b) and discussed in the literature sparked by it (see, e.g., Hawley 2018; Mikkola 2019; Schaffer 2019).

In the same spirit, one could argue that on the layperson's notion of war criminality, to be a war criminal just is to commit certain atrocities in a war context. And while it is true, in this sense, that Khan was a war criminal, this is not a legal fact, and so it is unsurprising that it doesn't require the existence of the Conventions in order for it to obtain. By contrast, on the technical notion defined by the Conventions, Khan was not, strictly speaking, a war criminal, precisely because that would have required laws that didn't exist at his time.

This reply might again be correct for some cases, but the problem is still that there is no guarantee that it will work in all of them. Specifically, it is a truism in legal theory and legal practice that there can be retroactive laws. That is, there can be – indeed, there are – laws that apply to events that took place prior to their coming into existence. And, it may be thought, this phenomenon – of which Khan's case is just a particularly controversial instance – is enough to generate Epstein-style scenarios.

However, and crucially, there are in fact (at least) two different ways of understanding retroactivity, and not all of them yield Epstein-cases. To stick with the same example, suppose for the sake of the argument that the Geneva Conventions of 1949 apply universally and retroactively (to all persons at all times), and that Khan's ordering the killing of civilians in Nishapur in 1221 satisfies the conditions they express. Then it presumably follows that Khan's actions in 1221 were war crimes, that is, that Khan was a war criminal. But notice that this is *not* yet sufficient to establish a case of TEMPORAL DISSONANCE since this requires not only that [Khan was a war criminal] and [Khan's actions in 1221 were war crimes] obtain *but that they do so before 1949*.

This is what we get if we adopt what I call a "static" understanding of retroactivity. On this interpretation, given the adoption of the Conventions, it was true at any time t starting from the atrocities, and not just after the enactment of the Conventions, that [Khan's actions in 1221 were war crimes] obtains at t. If this is the case – if the fact that Khan was a war criminal obtained before the Conventions were adopted – *then* we'd have a genuine instance of temporal disjointness between norm and fact. This view might be motivated by an eternalist temporal ontology according to which past, present, and future entities all exist and are equally real, coupled with the idea that the state of the world at one time can be metaphysically determined – though not grounded, on pain of violating SYNCHRONICITY – by a state of the world located at a later time.

Yet there is an alternative way of conceiving retroactivity that does not yield this result. On a "dynamic" conception of retroactivity, while it is now true that Khan was a war criminal, this was false before 1949. That is, until 1949 it was false that Khan's actions in 1221 were war crimes: these actions *became* war crimes when the Conventions were adopted. And if this is the correct understanding of the case, the cotemporality of norm and fact is regained (blocking the violation of SYNCHRONICITY), since [Khan was a war criminal] did not obtain before the Conventions became law.

This might perhaps be viewed as a more faithful representation of what our pretheoretical notion of retroactivity involves. Notice, however, that it appears to have the disturbing consequence that the past has changed. For one and the same fact about the past, namely [Khan's actions in 1221 were war crimes], did not obtain before 1949 and did obtain after that. While in 1500, say, it was false that Khan's atrocities in 1221 were war crimes, in 1950 it was true. It is unclear how problematic this ultimately is.[73] But if, as seems sensible, the past is settled and cannot change, then there are strong reasons to find a better solution.

The second premise expresses the principle that grounding is a synchronic relation, by stating that it relates only cotemporal entities. In the case of facts, it says that some facts ground another only if all the relata are temporally co-obtaining facts.[74] The advocate of M1–2 could reply by denying this premise, that is, by denying the synchronicity of grounding. At first sight, this reply may appear to be objectionably ad hoc. If violations of synchronicity only happen in the legal domain, then why should we revise our general conception of grounding? Why shouldn't we rather think that legal facts are simply not grounded in legal norms after all?

Probably the best answer here is to show that law is not the only domain exhibiting such failures, as other domains do too. Here, then, are some plausible cases. (Warning: The following claims embody controversial philosophical views. One doesn't need to agree with them, but merely appreciate that if they are true then they violate synchronicity, and if they are false – after all, they are contentious claims – then that has little to do with failures of synchronicity, since many of their philosophical rivals violate it too.) The moral fact that one now ought to φ is grounded in the past fact that one promised to φ, or in the future fact that φ-ing will cause the best overall consequences. The fact that Robin is the person she is is grounded in her psychological continuity with her earlier self. The fact that the sentence 'Caesar crossed the Rubicon' is now true is grounded in the past event of Caesar's crossing the Rubicon. The semantic fact that 'Robin' now refers to Robin holds in virtue of a past act of naming her in this way. The fact that 'water' now means water is grounded in causal-historical

---

[73] For discussions of similar cases, see Barlassina and Del Prete (2015), Brouwer (ms), Iacona (2016), and Torrengo (2018).

[74] The view that grounding is synchronic has been advocated by some authors (Leuenberger 2014b; Rosen 2010; Skiles 2015) and suggested by others (Bernstein 2016; Schaffer 2012, 2016), and is otherwise implicit in much theorizing about grounding and many of its applications. Among its chief motivations is probably the fact that grounding is as intimate a relation between numerically distinct entities as there can be (Fine 2012), or the idea that the grounded is "no addition of being," or nothing over and above its grounds (Schaffer 2009).

facts about the way the word was introduced, communicative chains of reference borrowing leading up to the present moment, and so on.[75]

The moral to be drawn from this is that while it may still be true that grounding – unlike causation – typically holds synchronically, this is not true in all cases.[76] In fact, by now there is a growing consensus that grounding may not always hold synchronically after all.[77] So the legal case may be seen as just another realm where diachronic grounding is manifested. It may then be open to the defender of M1–2 to accept a static interpretation of retroactivity, and yet to claim that this poses no threat to their view. The fact that Khan's actions in 1221 were war crimes obtains at t_1 in virtue of the laws of war that exist at t_2, by being retroactively grounded in them, and that's okay.

To conclude, it is worth noting that, independently of the difficult issues that arise in connection with the correct interpretation of retroactivity (i.e., whether it involves diachronic determination or rather changing the past), the legal domain also appears to exhibit *prospective* cases of diachronic grounding. These are cases in which a law regulating a legal property P *precedes* in time (and so is temporally disjoint from) a fact about the instantiation of P. For a toy case of this kind, consider the following. At t_1, Mary acquires the legal ownership of an estate *e* partly in virtue of a norm, valid at t_1, allowing her to purchase *e*. At a later time t_2, let us suppose, that law is repealed (the norm ceases to be valid), but the fact that Mary is the legal owner of *e* still holds.[78] So the fact [Mary has legal ownership over *e*] obtains at t_2, even though the law on the basis of which Mary acquired that property no longer exists. Some laws thus appear to "project" their effects into the future beyond the time at which they exist. For those who believe in diachronic grounding, these will be cases in which the legal facts are grounded in past laws.

3.7.3 The Modal Argument Against Explanatory Norms

In similar fashion, the modal argument takes the following shape:

MODAL DISSONANCE   For some world *w*, some legal fact of the form [F*a*] obtains at *w* and no legal norm of the form [L(φ, F)] obtains at *w*.

---

[75] Rosen (2017a) gives a different formulation of synchronicity, according to which some facts ground another fact only if they are all about the same temporal region, and provides plausible counterexamples. Indeed, if this is what is meant by the claim that grounding is synchronic, then a fortiori these counterexamples will work.

[76] Causation, by contrast, typically or necessarily holds diachronically, so this would still make for a disanalogy between constitutive and causal determination.

[77] Various authors have pointed out that synchronicity may be a mistaken assumption. See, e.g., Baron, Miller, and Tallant (2020), Bennett (2017), Correia and Merlo (2024), and Rosen (2017a).

[78] Thanks to Mark Greenberg for suggesting this example.

WORLDBOUND Γ grounds [p] only if all the facts Γ and [p] obtain at the same world w.

NO GROUND$_M$ Some legal fact of the form [Fa] is not grounded in any legal norm [L(φ, F)].

The same clarifications we made for the temporal argument apply here. First, the specification that 'no' legal norm should obtain at the same world as the legal fact it is about is due to the fact that there could be multiple norms regulating the legal properties at issue, some of which possibly have the same form. Second, while the conclusion that some legal fact is not grounded in any legal norm is not explicitly stated here, it follows from NO GROUND$_M$ together with the plausible premise that if any legal norm grounds [Fa], it is a legal norm of the form [L(φ, F)]. Third, the argument can easily be modified to target M3–4 instead.[79]

As before, the first premise should be supported by cases. Epstein (2015, 2019a, 2019b) provides them, one of which is analogous to the temporal case presented earlier. In one of its versions (Epstein 2019b: 237), he invites us to consider a possible world w that is just like the actual world @, except that it ends in 1500. In w too, then, Genghis Khan orders the slaughter of Nishapur in 1221. But unlike @, w hosts no Geneva Conventions, since the world ends before their enactment. Now suppose, again for the sake of the argument, that Khan's actual actions qualify as war crimes relative to the Conventions. If so, is Khan a war criminal in w?

Epstein holds that he is. For the Conventions are, in his words, a "universal" tool: they apply to all possible situations, regardless of whether they exist there (Epstein 2019a: 771). In other words, such norms modally "export," applying even to possible worlds in which they fail to exist.[80] If so, then [Khan is a war criminal] obtains at w, while the Geneva Conventions do not: some legal facts are modally disjoint from the norms that provide conditions for the instantiations of the legal properties they involve. Assume WORLDBOUND, and it follows that some legal facts aren't grounded in such norms.

---

[79] As for M3, one needs to substitute MODAL DISSONANCE with the claim that some fact of the form [[$\varphi(a)$] fully grounds [Fa]] obtains at a world at which [L(φ, F)] does not. From this it follows, via WORLDBOUND, that the former fact isn't grounded in the latter. As for M4, if we replace WORLDBOUND with the principle that metaphysical explanation only relates worldmate entities, it will follow, together with MODAL DISSONANCE, that [Fa] is not metaphysically explained by [L(φ, F)].

[80] Schaffer (2019) introduces the term 'exportation,' but applies it primarily to the relation that holds between rules and their metaphysical determinants (grounding for him, anchoring for Epstein). Derivatively, however, it can also be ascribed to rules themselves, to qualify those that "subsume" or "apply to" things that exist at different worlds and/or times.

3.7.4 Replies to the Modal Argument

As before, the argument is valid, so one needs to take issue with its premises. As before, one answer might consist in taking issue with the particular example. One could again distinguish between the ordinary and technical notions of war criminality, war criminal$_o$ and war criminal$_l$. In the ordinary sense, Khan *is* a war criminal$_o$ in *w*, since he committed atrocities there too, but this fails to vindicate MODAL DISSONANCE, since [Khan is a war criminal$_o$] is not a particular legal fact. And in the technical sense, [Khan is a war criminal$_l$] does not obtain at *w*, precisely because the relevant legal norms don't exist there.[81] Either the fact obtains but it isn't legal, or it is legal but it doesn't obtain. This way, we may still be able to vindicate some of the pull toward Epstein's cases (or some pull in the vicinity) without giving up on the claim that norms ground facts.

Again, this much could be fine. But remember that the advocate of the argument needs just one case of modal exportation, and it could be doubted that this divide-and-conquer strategy generalizes to all cases. So this reply fails to give us a general reason to believe that MODAL DISSONANCE is never instantiated. And, one may wonder, is it really *impossible* for there to be rules with unrestricted modal scope? That is, can there really be no rule whose scope of application ranges over all possible actions, regardless of where in logical space they take place, and regardless of whether the rule itself exists there? These, I take it, are difficult questions. As there is no obvious analogue of retroactivity in the modal case, the burden should presumably lie with the proponent of the argument to come up with plausible instances of this phenomenon.

An alternative way of denying the first premise, both in the modal and in the temporal case, could appeal to a fact about the nature of legal norms. Legal norms, one might think, are what is sometimes called "created abstracta": they are abstract objects created by us.[82] Because they are created, they begin to exist *at* a certain point in time (and at a certain world). Yet because they are abstract, they do not exist *in* space or time. Combining these two insights, one may claim that once a legal norm is created, it exists *at all* times and worlds, even though it doesn't exist *in any* time or world. This view is admittedly elusive, and would need much refinement. But notice that if one manages to develop this idea, it

---

[81] This response resembles Schaffer's (2019) definition reply. On this reply, at the actual world the term 'war criminal' is stipulated to apply to every possible case where the relevant atrocities occur, so the stipulative definition does "export." But this is unproblematic, for legal rules play no role in the metaphysical explanation of the relevant fact, and so they need not export. In our terminology, the fact in question is not a *legal* fact, and so legal norms need not play any role in explaining it.

[82] On the metaphysics of created abstracta, see, e.g., Thomasson (1998).

may thwart both arguments by establishing that norms and facts do co-obtain, both temporally and modally.

But suppose that the preceding replies fail, and that MODAL DISSONANCE is true.[83] What, then, are the prospects of denying WORLDBOUND? WORLDBOUND says that if some facts ground another fact, then these facts must all be worldmates. We can therefore think of this as a modal extension of the principle that grounding is a factive relation. Whereas factivity says that Γ grounds [p] at @ only if Γ and [p] all obtain at @, WORLDBOUND extends this to all possible worlds.

WORLDBOUND has so far received little treatment (or endorsement) in the literature, so there is an especially open path for the proponent of M1–2 to deny it. In fact, Schaffer (2019) explicitly rejects it, and holds that grounding can hold across worlds, as in the case of Khan and other similar social facts.[84] In this spirit, it could be maintained that [Khan is a war criminal] obtains at w in virtue of the Geneva Conventions that exist at @, by means of being grounded in them.

Carving out a legal exception to a general principle of grounding theory may, however, seem suspiciously ad hoc. So it would be good if there were also nonlegal cases that counterexample it. Consider the following. At @, [It is possible that p] obtains. Why, you may ask? A natural answer might be that [It is possible that p] obtains at @ because [p] obtains at w, namely, one of the worlds where p is the case. Just as existential generalizations of the form [$\exists x Fx$] are grounded in their instances [Fa],[85] one may hold that possibility facts at a world are grounded in facts that obtain at worlds where those possibilities are realized.[86]

So it is doubtful that the unrestricted version of WORLDBOUND holds. Still, given the nature of the counterexample, one might think that exceptions to it will be found exclusively when dealing with modal facts. Generalizing from this, one might think that cross-world grounding is allowed only when some of the facts that stand in it are modal facts. This licenses a new restricted principle along the following lines:

WORLDBOUND* For any nonmodal facts Γ, [p]: if Γ ground [p], then all the facts Γ and [p] obtain at the same world w.

---

[83] Schaffer (2019), for instance, is happy to concede as much.
[84] We'll come back to the details shortly.   [85] See, e.g., Fine (2012) and Rosen (2010).
[86] Similarly, just as accidental generalizations are grounded in their worldmate instances, necessity facts could perhaps be cross-worldly explained by all their otherworldly instances. This, however, is more controversial, as some authors (see again Fine 2012; Rosen 2010) take necessity facts to be grounded in essences.

Once this principle is substituted in the original argument in place of WORLDBOUND, the key question becomes whether the facts that concern us here are modal facts or not (since the new modal argument will succeed only if they are nonmodal).

This raises the question of what counts as a (non)modal fact. Plausibly, the notions of a modal fact and a nonmodal fact are mutually exclusive and jointly exhaustive. Every fact is either modal or nonmodal, and no fact is both modal and nonmodal. Let us propose that [*p*] is a modal fact at *w* iff some of its constituents are "about" worlds other than *w*. Consequently, [*p*] is a nonmodal fact at *w* iff all of its constituents are about *w*.

The key aspect of this definition is that modality becomes a world-relative affair. A fact may count as a modal fact at a world, and fail to count as a modal fact at another. Still, some facts will count as modal at all worlds. For instance, [It is possible that *p*] will be a modal fact at every world simply because some of its constituents involve other possibilities no matter where it obtains.

What about particular legal facts? Is [Khan is a war criminal] a modal fact, according to this definition? When we consider it as obtaining at the actual world it doesn't seem to be one, since both Khan and the property of being a war criminal are "actual things." When we consider it as obtaining at *w*, however, things become less clear. Khan clearly exists at *w*, so there is no doubt here. But what about the property *war criminal*, whose satisfaction conditions reside in the actual world, and not at *w*?

Schaffer (2019) gives us a recipe to count particular legal facts such as this one as modal. He holds that legal properties such as being a war criminal are not really the monadic properties they seem to be. Rather, they are relations to rules. In this case, the property truly expressed by 'is a war criminal' is not the monadic property of being a war criminal *simpliciter*, but rather the relational property of *being a war criminal relative to the Geneva Conventions of 1949*. Similarly, the property of having the right to vote in US elections is really the relational property of *having the right to vote in US elections relative to voting norm N*. And so on for any other legal property or relation.[87]

Applying Schaffer's insight across the board leads to *relationalism*, that is, the view that all particular legal facts are relational facts. According to relationalism, strictly speaking, there are no such facts as [Esther has the right to vote in US elections], [Robin and Andrea are legally married], or [Whitey Bulger is a first-degree murderer]. For since the properties they involve are relational to the rules about them, these facts are incomplete, missing an empty

---

[87] In the case of relations, for any apparently *n*-place relation we might consider, the view says that it is in fact an *n*+1-place relation, with the extra slot occupied by the legal norm that regulates it.

slot. Instead, the real counterparts of these "facts" are [Esther has the right to vote in US elections relative to US law], [Robin and Andrea are legally married relative to Spanish law], [Whitey Bulger is a first-degree murderer relative to the Massachusetts General Laws], and so on.

If this view about the nature of particular legal facts is correct, then some legal facts can be modal facts. When [Khan is a war criminal relative to the Geneva Conventions] obtains at *w*, for instance, it is a modal fact since it is partly about the Geneva Conventions of @, and so it is partly about a world other than *w*. As a consequence, it can be grounded in the Conventions existing at @ without violating WORLDBOUND*.[88]

This strategy, then, blocks the modal argument by rejecting WORLDBOUND, making room for the possibility of cross-world grounding when modal facts are involved, and by holding that the problematic cases of particular legal facts are indeed modal facts. It bears emphasis, however, that each of these steps can be challenged, so it is unclear whether M1–4 ultimately withstand this argument.[89]

3.8 Nonexplanatory Norms: Model 5

If all the preceding accounts are inadequate, then perhaps we ought to reject the view that legal norms are explanatory. Even though it seems as though legal norms contribute to the metaphysical explanation of legal facts (or of grounding facts about them), they are in fact explanatorily inert generalizations. The resulting view, M5, holds, like M3–4, that legal facts are fully grounded in base facts. The fact that Esther has the right to vote in elections, for instance, is fully grounded in the fact that she is an eighteen-year-old US citizen. But, unlike M3–4, M5 maintains that legal norms are mere *summaries* of grounding patterns involving legal properties and base conditions.[90] Legal norms, on this view, don't *govern* the explanatory connections that tie legal properties together with the underlying properties that ground them. Rather, they merely *report* grounding conditions for the instantiation of legal properties and relations. Because of this, they can unproblematically take the form of [FG-LAW], stating

---

[88] More generally, Schaffer (2019: 763) holds that "the grounds for a grounded output must be present at the time, place, and world *when the grounded output is intrinsic*. But when the grounded output involves an extrinsic, relational property, involving a relation to the goings-on at another time, place, and/or world, part of its grounds will be found at that other time, place, and/or world."

[89] As Schaffer (2019) and Epstein (2019a) point out, viewing legal properties and facts as relational and modal is a revisionary stance vis-à-vis common sense. For an in-depth treatment of the topics in this section, see Chilovi (2025).

[90] Berker (2019) and Epstein (2015) advocate the analogue of M5 for moral principles and social rules respectively.

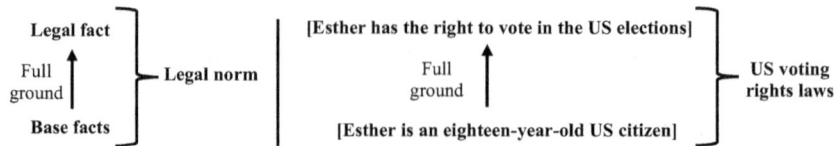

Figure 6 Model 5: In general and applied to a case.

that if anything meets certain conditions, then this *fully* grounds the instantiation of a legal property or relation (see Figure 6).

It is worth noting that legal norms, thus understood, can still play a valuable *epistemic* role in explaining – that is, in knowing or figuring out – what legal facts obtain. For instance, knowing that anyone with a certain age and citizenship thereby has the right to vote will allow one to infer whether someone is legally entitled to vote from their age and citizenship. In fact, it is hard to see how knowledge of legal facts could be acquired at all in the absence of knowledge of the relevant norms. So they would not only be useful for gaining knowledge of legal facts, but would be indispensable for it. For this reason, although M5 explains *away* the appearance that legal norms metaphysically explain legal facts, it still assigns a meaningful epistemic explanatory role to them. To this extent, there may still be a sense in which M5 fulfills the desideratum of vindicating norms' apparent role in explanation, though this remains to be seen.

To illustrate M5 in more detail, let me present its most elaborate implementation in the literature, namely Epstein's (2015, 2019a, 2019b) account of social (legal) facts. Epstein's view is constructed around two main building blocks. First, lawmaking facts, such as facts about the enactment of statutes, judicial decisions, and the like metaphysically determine legal norms, which Epstein calls "frame principles."[91] Frame principles do not govern the production of legal facts or the grounding relations between legal facts and base facts. Rather, they summarize the grounding conditions of instantiation for legal properties and relations, and thereby express ways in which legal facts are grounded. Formally, frame principles can be modeled as functions from worlds to worlds. The frame principle that sets out conditions for voting rights, for instance, is the function that, given as input a world where Esther is an eighteen-year-old US citizen, returns a world where this fact grounds the fact that Esther has the right to vote in US elections. The set of all frame principles is what Epstein calls a "frame."[92]

---

[91] This presentation of possible lawmaking facts is merely illustrative. According to Epstein, the relation between legal norms and their determinants is not grounding, but rather a different metaphysical relation that he calls 'anchoring.'

[92] On Epstein's view, social rules are also frame principles, so frames will include these too. However, here we focus solely on the frame principles that are legal, and consequently solely on "legal frames."

Second, relations of full ground between legal facts and base facts unfold in the ways codified in the frame principles set up by lawmaking facts. One way of thinking about this is to imagine lawmaking facts as constructing a scaffold within which legal facts arise from base facts. Once lawmaking facts set up conditions for the instantiation of a legal property, facts about the satisfaction of these conditions give rise to legal facts. In a sense, frame principles are like lenses we use to "see" what legal facts there are at a world, given the base facts that obtain there. If, say, we look at a world w through the lenses of present-day US law, then if Esther is an eighteen-year-old US citizen at w, we should also see that Esther has the right to vote at w. If the frame through which we look at w is different, then, even given the same set of base facts, we might see different legal facts to be generated at it.

It could be doubted whether the epistemic role assigned to norms by M5 adequately vindicates norms' apparent role in explanation. But whatever one thinks about this issue, there is also another challenge the account faces: a challenge that it shares with any view on which base facts are the full grounds of legal facts (including M3–4). We noticed at the beginning that there is a powerful argument against these views (and, correlatively, in favor of accounts that are premised on their denial, i.e., M1–2). The problem is that the claim that base facts are full grounds of legal facts appears to lead to a failure of GROUNDING NECESSITARIANISM. For recall that given GROUNDING NECESSITARIANISM, it follows that if some base facts fully ground a legal fact at @, then any world where the former facts obtain is a world where the latter fact does, and this seems clearly false. For instance, in a world in which US voting laws set the minimum age at twenty-one, eighteen-year-old Esther intuitively does *not* have the right to vote, even though she would have that right at @. How can views that take base facts as full grounds of legal facts address this challenge?

One possibility is to preserve GROUNDING NECESSITARIANISM by claiming that, despite appearances, legal facts that are actually fully grounded in some base facts obtain at any world where those base facts are present. What needs to be acknowledged is that the *lawmaking facts* are contingent. In the actual world, lawmaking facts set up the conditions for having the right to vote (being a first-degree murder, being a war criminal, etc.) as they do, but they could easily have been different, and could easily be superseded by new ones. Yet, crucially, this does not mean that in worlds where the lawmaking facts are different, the particular legal facts that obtain in the actual world fail to obtain.

On the way of developing this strategy pursued by Epstein (2015), this is so because legal norms are modal principles endowed with unrestricted necessity, quantifying over all possible worlds irrespective of whether the lawmaking facts that set them up in the actual world exist there.[93] If this is the scope that legal norms have, then they guarantee that base facts ground legal facts even at worlds where such lawmaking facts fail to obtain (unless their presence is required by the instantiation conditions included in the legal norms themselves). For instance, laws of war criminality might say that, necessarily, if someone commits certain atrocities during a war, that grounds the fact that they are a war criminal, where the necessity operator is unrestricted (see Epstein 2019b: 234). If so, then Khan would be a war criminal in every world where he commits the relevant atrocities, no matter whether the Geneva Conventions are enacted there.

One objection to this view is that while it might be defensible to assign this modal strength to some legal norms (such as the laws of war), it will be less plausible for others. For instance, it is odd to think that eighteen-year-old Esther has the right to vote in worlds where the voting laws set the minimum age at twenty-one just because in the actual world the voting laws grant her that right.[94] In other words, the problem is that at least some legal facts appear to be modally sensitive not only to their base facts but also to lawmaking facts, such that had those been different, different legal facts would have obtained.

In response, one might secure a sense in which legal facts are modally sensitive to lawmaking facts, by drawing on the distinction, familiar from two-dimensional semantics, between worlds considered as actual and worlds considered as counterfactual (Epstein 2015: 119). In particular, although on this view Esther has the right to vote even at worlds where the lawmaking facts are different, it is still true that if the *actual* world had been different (if different legal norms had been actual), then she may not have had that right (at this or other worlds). More generally, given what lawmaking facts there actually are, the frame principles associated with them apply universally across modal space. But if the actual laws had been different, or if they were to change, then different frames would have been, or will be, (unrestrictedly) applicable.

If this response seems too actuality-centric, one could allow for a different kind of frame-dependence that eliminates the apparent bias in favor of (frames set up at) the actual world. In this vein, one could hold that different frames can be set up at different worlds, and that the question of what legal facts obtain is a matter that can be settled only relative to a frame of choice, without this having to be the actual frame. Given a frame f set up at a "pinned" world w_p, the legal facts that obtain at *any* world w are those that arise, given the base facts that obtain at w, in

---

[93] See Epstein (2015: 116, and fn. 1).
[94] Mikkola (2015: 791) and Schaffer (2019: 757) make a parallel point with respect to facts about money.

accordance with the conditions set out by f at w_p. Yet given a different choice of frame, different legal facts can be "seen" to obtain at every world.[95]

A different way of making plausible the idea that actual base facts ground the corresponding legal facts even at worlds with different laws is to appeal to a form of relationalism about legal facts and properties. In this vein, as we saw, Schaffer (2019) has argued that social features are relative to rules. For instance, the apparent monadic property of being a war criminal is really a two-place relation that holds between certain individual people and the Geneva Convention of 1949. More generally, given an apparent n-place social feature F, F is really an $n+1$-place feature, F relative to N, where N is a slot to be filled by a set of norms that provide grounding conditions for its instantiation.[96] If legal features involve relations to rules, then it is less counterintuitive to think that they can be instantiated at worlds where the actual laws are absent. At worlds where the age requirements are set at twenty-one, for instance, eighteen-year-old Esther still possesses the right to vote *relative to actual present-day US law*. (Of course, she won't be able to exercise that right, but that is a different issue.) In general, given a law that sets conditions for the instantiation of a legal feature, it is not so implausible that one can possess that feature relative to the law in question at contexts where the laws are different.

Finally, the last reply available to the advocate of M5 (and M3–4) is to reject GROUNDING NECESSITARIANISM and claim that grounding is a contingent relation.[97] At the actual world, Esther has the right to vote wholly in virtue of the fact that she's an eighteen-year-old US citizen, yet at worlds where the voting laws are different, she lacks that right despite having the same age and citizenship she has here. The modal scope of legal norms is accordingly viewed as restricted, though there are different options as to how the restriction can be modeled. A legal norm N may be taken to apply only to worlds in which N is set up (or only in worlds where N exists); or N could apply to *some* worlds beyond those in which it exists, without it extending to all worlds; and so on. One could even be a pluralist about the modal scope of legal norms, and think that some norms "export" to worlds beyond those where they exist, while others do not, so that the question of modal scope will need to be settled on a case-by-case basis.

Whichever choice is made here, it is worth emphasizing that on this view, grounding will not in general necessitate. Legal facts that are fully grounded at the actual world in some base facts can fail to obtain at worlds where the same base facts obtain yet the norms are different, if those norms' modal scope is restricted. However, proponents of this view can still hold on to a restricted version of necessitation, namely that base facts necessitate legal facts *within the*

---

[95] Thanks to Brian Epstein for discussion of this point.
[96] Schaffer (2019) defends relationalism about social features.
[97] See Leuenberger (2014b) and Skiles (2015).

relevant frame (Schaffer 2019: 757). That is, if the norms' scope, while not completely unrestricted, extends beyond the actual world, then base facts will necessitate the corresponding legal facts within the frame projected by those norms. Whether this kind of connection between grounding and necessity is strong enough is a matter that needs further exploration.

3.9 No Legal Norms: Model 0

All the models that we have discussed presuppose the existence of laws or legal norms, understood as general standards that connect legal relations with the underlying features responsible for explaining them. This is a natural assumption to make. On a widespread view, legal norms make up the law of a legal system, and play a critical role for laypeople, lawyers, and legal philosophers alike. To the layperson, they provide action guidance and serve as grounds of praise, and for criticizing (non)compliance. To lawyers, they constitute one object of discovery in courtroom disputes, the target of legal interpretation, and a key premise in inferences to conclusions about the legal properties of individuals.[98] To legal philosophers working in general jurisprudence, they constitute the target inquiry, with positivists and nonpositivists making competing claims about their nature and grounds.

Yet their existence can be challenged in various ways. First, one might be skeptical of their existence on the basis of a general opposition to abstract objects. Legal norms are not identical to concrete acts of lawmaking or to legal texts. They are determined by such things, to be sure, but they can survive changes that the latter cannot, and cannot be perceived. Rather, one plausible way to think of them is as "created" or "dependent" abstracta.[99] Legal norms are complex abstract objects, composed of normative contents bearing the relation of legal validity to legal systems. Since they come to stand in the validity relation in virtue of contingent social facts, they exhibit temporal duration, unlike ordinary abstract objects. And since they bear this relation to legal systems, they can be thought of as having some sort of spatial location. Still, their abstract nature makes their ontological status open to the worries that apply to abstract objects in general.[100]

Second, one could harbor particularist scruples. Legal norms are supposed to provide general, exceptionless connections between base conditions and legal facts, such that if the former are satisfied, the latter obtain. One, however, could be skeptical that any such connections exist that are not hopelessly gerrymandered or tediously long. Alleged truths of that sort, the particularist claims,

---

[98] On a standard view, to apply the law is to subsume the facts of the case under general norms (see, e.g., Moreso and Chilovi 2018).
[99] Compare with Thomasson's (1998) theory of fictional characters as dependent abstracta.
[100] See Falguera, Martínez-Vidal, and Rosen (2022) and Rodriguez-Pereyra (2019).

always, or nearly always, admit of exceptions, and so the most we can get are rough approximations that never truly hold in full generality.

Third, one might have reservations on account of parsimony, arguing for the elimination of legal norms from the fact that they don't do any important work in our theories. As we saw when dealing with M5, it could be disputed whether legal norms play any role in metaphysical explanations. Moreover, while this is consistent with legal norms playing an epistemic role in reasoning to legal facts, this too can be challenged. A different option is to suggest that we can derive the legal facts from the base facts in combination with the things – let us call them the 'legal determinants' – that are normally thought to determine the legal norms, *without passing through those norms*. Rather than thinking that statutory provisions, judicial decisions, and the like determine something called "the law," which then determines the legal facts, another possibility is to cut out this middle level entirely. Perhaps we don't need to first determine the content of the law, in order to then infer the legal properties of individuals, but could instead establish those properties on the basis of the legal determinants directly.[101] If legal norms are explanatorily inert both metaphysically and epistemically, then why not eliminate them altogether? To posit unnecessary entities of this sort would be a clear violation of Ockham's injunction not to multiply entities beyond necessity.

Notice the subtle difference between this view and others we have discussed. If, as is often assumed, grounding is a transitive relation,[102] then there is a sense in which even models on which legal facts are explained by norms can ultimately dispense with those norms, for any explanation of legal facts by norms could be replaced by one that is just as complete, yet appeals to the grounds of the legal norms instead. Here, by contrast, legal norms are not thought to play even a mediate role in (metaphysical or epistemic) explanation, and this is regarded as a reason to eliminate them.

A picture of this sort, which does away with law and focuses on legal relations instead, has been recently advocated by several authors.[103] It also

---

[101] Kornhauser (ms) makes this argumentative move in favor of eliminativism about law, and Murphy (2014) discusses it. This position should be distinguished from views that take law to be a branch of morality, and from views that take legal relations to be moral and deny that there is a distinctively legal normative kind. See Hershovitz (2023) for the latter view.

[102] For discussion, see the references in fn. 38.

[103] Kornhauser (ms) is the foremost advocate of eliminativism about law, and credits Dworkin as a proto-eliminativist. He argues that we should dispense with the notion of law, and focus on the determination of legal relations instead. His view is discussed by Murphy (2008, 2014), who rejects eliminativism. Dworkin (2011), Greenberg (2014), and Hershovitz (2015, 2023) all argue against there being a distinctively legal domain of nonmoral normativity, and argue that law is not a separate normative system from morality. However, these latter authors are not eliminativists in the strong sense of denying that law exists; rather, they view it as a branch of morality (see fn. 2). Hershovitz holds the deflationary view that there is no genuine question of what the law is, since a number of different questions correspond to different senses of 'law,'

appears to have been adumbrated in parts of Dworkin's work, especially in passages such as the following:

> I hope to persuade lawyers to lay the entire picture of existing law aside in favour of a theory of law that takes questions about legal rights as special questions about political rights, so that one may think a plaintiff has a certain legal right without supposing that any rule or principle that already 'exists' provides that right. In place of the misleading question, whether judges find rules in the 'existing law' or make up rules not to be found there, we must ask whether judges try to determine what the parties have a right to have, or whether they create what they take to be new rights to serve social goals. (Dworkin 1977: 293)

The view – M0 – that results from this eliminativist position explains legal facts without any appeal to norms. Unlike in M5, according to this model, base facts aren't the full grounds of legal facts. Rather, legal facts are grounded also in the sorts of facts that, according to all other views, are responsible for determining legal norms (see Figure 7).

The exact nature of the legal determinants is one of the central questions in general jurisprudence, and it needn't concern us here. These uncontroversially include things like legal texts, statutory enactments, judicial decisions, and the actions and mental states of lawmakers. They might also (more controversially) include social rules and conventions, or moral facts and principles. Legal positivists and nonpositivists disagree on what the legal determinants are, for example on whether they are wholly social or partly moral in character. And although this issue is usually framed as concerning the grounds of *law*, notice that for someone who opts for M0 and eliminativism about law, the same dividing lines and theoretical options with regard to the determination of law can be reframed as having to do with the determination of legal facts instead.

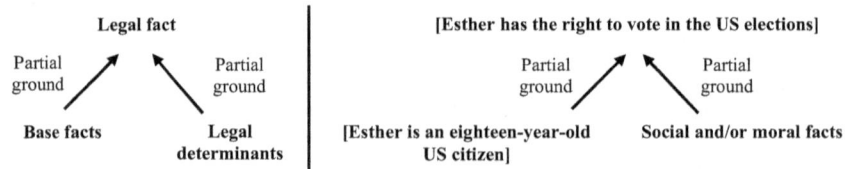

Figure 7 Model 0: General and applied to a case.

---

and Nye (2022, 2024) holds that we should stop talking about law. For discussion, see Chilovi (2024). Dworkin, Hershovitz, Kornhauser, and Nye all hold in different ways that our theories should focus on the legal rights and obligations of individuals directly, instead of trying to get there by engaging in endless questions about the nature of law. For discussion, see also Crummey and Pavlakos (2024).

The key point for our purposes is that, according to M0, the legal determinants determine the legal facts directly, acting as immediate partial grounds of those facts, without going through law as an intermediary.

4 Conclusion

This Element has dealt with an undertheorized question in the metaphysics of law, namely how facts about the legal properties and relations of particulars (such as their rights, duties, powers, etc.) are metaphysically explained. We broke down this question into two separate issues. First, we examined the nature of the explanatory relation connecting legal facts to their metaphysical determinants. Second, we inquired into the kinds of entities that figure in the explanation of legal facts. In doing so, we paid special attention to the role that laws, or legal norms, play in such explanations. As it turns out, there are several different ways that legal facts might be explained, all of which have something to be said in their favor, and none of which is immune from problems. Along the way, we also touched on a number of further issues bearing on our main topics. These further issues have to do with the nature of metaphysical grounding, the relation between grounding and explanation, the logical form of legal norms, the modal profile of legal facts, and the retroactivity of laws.

References

Amijee, F. (2020). Principle of sufficient reason. In M. J. Raven (ed.), *The Routledge Handbook of Metaphysical Grounding*. New York: Routledge, pp. 63–75.

Atiq, E. H. (2020). There are no easy counterexamples to legal anti-positivism. *Journal of Ethics and Social Philosophy*, 17(1), 1–26.

Audi, P. (2012). Grounding: Toward a theory of the in-virtue-of relation. *Journal of Philosophy*, 109(12), 685–711.

Barlassina, L. and Del Prete, F. (2015). The puzzle of the changing past. *Analysis*, 75(1), 59–67.

Baron, S., Miller, K. and Tallant, J. (2020). Grounding at a distance. *Philosophical Studies*, 177(11), 3373–90.

Bennett, K. (2011). By our bootstraps. *Philosophical Perspectives*, 25, 27–41.

Bennett, K. (2017). *Making Things Up*. Oxford: Oxford University Press.

Berker, S. (2018). The unity of grounding. *Mind*, 127(507), 729–77.

Berker, S. (2019). The explanatory ambitions of moral principles. *Noûs*, 53(4), 904–36.

Berman, M. (2018). Our principled constitution. *University of Pennsylvania Law Review*, 166(6), 1325–414.

Berman, M. (2021). Dworkin versus Hart revisited: The challenge of non-lexical determination. *Oxford Journal of Legal Studies*, 42(2), 548–77.

Berman, M. (2024). How practices make principles and how principles make rules. *Journal of Ethics and Social Philosophy*, 28(3), 299–356.

Bernstein, S. (2016). Grounding is not causation. *Philosophical Perspectives*, 30, 21–38.

Bliss, R. (2014). Viciousness and circles of ground. *Metaphilosophy*, 45(2), 245–56.

Brouwer, T. (ms). Changing the social past.

Castañeda, H.-N. (1984). Causes, causity, and energy. *Midwest Studies in Philosophy*, 9(1), 17–27.

Chalmers, D. J. (1996). *The Conscious Mind: In Search of a Fundamental Theory*. Oxford: Oxford University Press.

Chilovi, S. (2020). Grounding-based formulations of legal positivism. *Philosophical Studies*, 177(11), 3283–302.

Chilovi, S. (2021). Grounding entails supervenience. *Synthese*, 198(Suppl. 6), 1317–34.

Chilovi, S. (2024). Normative monism and radical deflationism. *Jurisprudence*, 15(2), 182–93.

Chilovi, S. (2025). Anchoring, grounding, and explanatory laws, *Inquiry*, 1–21.

Chilovi, S. and Pavlakos, G. (2019). Law-determination as grounding: A common grounding framework for jurisprudence. *Legal Theory*, 25(1), 53–76.

Chilovi, S. and Pavlakos, G. (2022). The explanatory demands of grounding in law. *Pacific Philosophical Quarterly*, 103(4), 900–33.

Chilovi, S. and Wodak, D. (2022). On the (in)significance of Hume's Law. *Philosophical Studies*, 179(2), 633–53.

Coleman, J. (2001). *Practice of Principle: In Defence of a Pragmatist Approach to Legal Theory*. Oxford: Oxford University Press.

Corkum, P. (2016). Ontological dependence and grounding in Aristotle. In *The Oxford Handbook of Topics in Philosophy* (online ed., Oxford Academic, April 1, 2014), https://doi.org/10.1093/oxfordhb/9780199935314.013.31.

Corkum, P. (2020). Ancient. In M. J. Raven (ed.), *The Routledge Handbook of Metaphysical Grounding*. New York: Routledge, pp. 20–32.

Correia, F. (2005). *Existential Dependence and Cognate Notions*. Munich: Philosophia.

Correia, F. (2010). Grounding and truth-functions. *Logique et Analyse*, 53(211), 251–79.

Correia, F. (2018). The logic of relative fundamentality. *Synthese*, 198(Suppl. 6), 1279–301.

Correia, F. and Merlo, G. (2024). Cross-temporal grounding. *Analytic Philosophy*, 65(3), 333–52.

Correia, F. and Schnieder, B. (2012). Grounding: An opinionated introduction. In F. Correia and B. Schnieder (eds.), *Metaphysical Grounding: Understanding the Structure of Reality*. Cambridge: Cambridge University Press, pp. 1–36.

Crummey, C. and Pavlakos, G. (2024). Not a set of norms or a set of practices. *Jurisprudence*, 15(2), 135–44.

Dancy, J. (1981). On moral properties. *Mind*, 90(359), 367–85.

Dasgupta, S. (2014a). The possibility of physicalism. *Journal of Philosophy*, 111(9/10), 557–92.

Dasgupta, S. (2014b). On the plurality of grounds. *Philosophers' Imprint*, 14, art. 20.

Dasgupta, S. (2017). Constitutive explanation. *Philosophical Perspectives*, 27, 74–97.

Davidson, D. (1967). Causal relations. *Journal of Philosophy*, 64(21), 691–703.

DePaul, M. R. (1987). Supervenience and moral dependence. *Philosophical Studies*, 51(3), 425–39.

deRosset, L. (2013). Grounding explanations. *Philosophers' Imprint*, 13, art. 7.

deRosset, L. (2025). Legal grounds. *Noûs*, 1–26. https://doi.org/10.1111/nous.12553.

Dworkin, R. (ed.) (1977). *Taking Rights Seriously*. London: Duckworth.

Dworkin, R. (1986). *Law's Empire*. Cambridge, MA: Harvard University Press.

Dworkin, R. (2011). *Justice for Hedgehogs*. Cambridge, MA: Harvard University Press.

Enoch, D. (2011). *Taking Morality Seriously: A Defense of Robust Realism*. Oxford: Oxford University Press.

Enoch, D. (2019). How principles ground. *Oxford Studies in Metaethics*, 14, 1–22.

Epstein, B. (2015). *The Ant Trap: Rebuilding the Foundations of the Social Sciences*. Oxford: Oxford University Press.

Epstein, B. (2019a). Anchoring versus grounding: Reply to Schaffer. *Philosophy and Phenomenological Research*, 99(3), 768–81.

Epstein, B. (2019b). Replies to Hawley, Mikkola, and Hindriks. *Inquiry*, 62(2), 230–46.

Fair, D. (1979). Causation and the flow of energy. *Erkenntnis*, 14(3), 219–50.

Falguera, J. L., Martínez-Vidal, C. and Rosen, G. (2022). Abstract objects. In E. N. Zalta (ed.), *The Stanford Encyclopedia of Philosophy* (online ed., Summer 2022, revised August 9, 2021). https://plato.stanford.edu/archives/sum2022/entries/abstract-objects/.

Fine, K. (1994). Essence and modality. *Philosophical Perspectives*, 8, 1–16.

Fine, K. (1995). Ontological dependence. *Proceedings of the Aristotelian Society*, 95(1), 269–90.

Fine, K. (2001). The question of realism. *Philosophers' Imprint*, 1, art. 1.

Fine, K. (2010). Some puzzles of ground. *Notre Dame Journal of Formal Logic*, 51(1), 97–118.

Fine, K. (2012). Guide to ground. In F. Correia and B. Schnieder (eds.), *Metaphysical Grounding: Understanding the Structure of Reality*. Cambridge: Cambridge University Press, pp. 37–80.

Finnis, J. (1979). *Natural Law and Natural Rights*. Oxford: Oxford University Press.

Gardner, J. (2001). Legal positivism: 5½ myths. *American Journal of Jurisprudence*, 46(1), 199–227.

Glazier, M. (2016). Laws and the completeness of the fundamental. In M. Jago (ed.), *Reality Making*. Oxford: Oxford University Press, pp. 11–37.

Greenberg, M. (2004). How facts make law. *Legal Theory*, 10(3), 157–98.

Greenberg, M. (2006). Hartian positivism and normative facts: How facts make law II. In S. Hershovitz (ed.), *Exploring Law's Empire: The Jurisprudence of Ronald Dworkin*. Oxford: Oxford University Press, pp. 265–90.

Greenberg, M. (2014). The moral impact theory of law. *Yale Law Journal*, 123(5), 1288–343.

Hart, H. L. A. (1961). *The Concept of Law*. Oxford: Oxford University Press.

Haukioja, J. (2017). Externalism and internalism. In C. Wright, B. Hale and A. Miller (eds.), *A Companion to the Philosophy of Language*, 2nd ed. Oxford: Blackwell, pp. 865–80.

Hawley, K. (2018). Comments on Brian Epstein's *The Ant Trap*. *Inquiry*, 62(2), 217–29.

Hempel, C. G. and Oppenheim, P. (1948). Studies in the logic of explanation. *Philosophy of Science*, 15(2), 135–75.

Hershovitz, S. (2015). The end of jurisprudence. *Yale Law Journal*, 124(4), 1160–205.

Hershovitz, S. (2023). *Law Is a Moral Practice*. Cambridge, MA: Harvard University Press.

Iacona, A. (2016). On the puzzle of the changing past. *Philosophia*, 44(1), 137–42.

Jackson, F. (1998). *From Metaphysics to Ethics: A Defence of Conceptual Analysis*. Oxford: Oxford University Press.

Jenkins, C. (2011). Is metaphysical dependence irreflexive? *The Monist*, 94(2), 267–76.

Kallestrup, J. (2012). *Semantic Externalism*. London: Routledge.

Kornhauser, L. A. (ms). Doing without the concept of law. NYU School of Law, Public Law Research Paper No. 15–33, August 3, 2015. http://dx.doi.org/10.2139/ssrn.2640605.

Koslicki, K. (2015). The coarse-grainedness of grounding. *Oxford Studies in Metaphysics*, 9, 306–44.

Kovacs, D. M. (2018). What is wrong with self-grounding? *Erkenntnis*, 83(6), 1157–80.

Kovacs, D. M. (2019). The myth of the myth of supervenience. *Philosophical Studies*, 176(8), 1967–89.

Kovacs, D. M. (2020). Modality. In M. J. Raven (ed.), *The Routledge Handbook of Metaphysical Grounding*. New York: Routledge, pp. 348–60.

Krämer, S. (2013). A simpler puzzle of ground. *Thought*, 2(2), 85–9.

Leiter, B. (2007). *Naturalizing Jurisprudence: Essays on American Legal Realism and Naturalism in Legal Philosophy*. Oxford: Oxford University Press.

Leuenberger, S. (2014a). From grounding to supervenience? *Erkenntnis*, 79(1), 227–40.

Leuenberger, S. (2014b). Grounding and necessity. *Inquiry*, 57(2), 151–74.

Lewis, D. (1983). New work for a theory of universals. *Australasian Journal of Philosophy*, 61(4), 343–77.

Lewis, D. (1994). Reduction of mind. In S. Guttenplan (ed.), *A Companion to the Philosophy of Mind*. Oxford: Blackwell, pp. 412–31.

Litland, J. E. (2013). On some counterexamples to the transitivity of grounding. *Essays in Philosophy*, 14(1), 19–32.

Litland, J. E. (2015). Grounding, explanation, and the limit of internality. *Philosophical Review*, 124(4), 481–532.

Litland, J. E. (2017). Grounding ground. *Oxford Studies in Metaphysics*, 10, 279–99.

López de Sa, D. (2009). Disjunctions, conjunctions, and their truthmakers. *Mind*, 118(470), 417–25.

Loss, R. (2016). Grounds, roots, and abysses. *Thought*, 5(1), 41–52.

Loss, R. (2017). Grounding, contingency, and transitivity. *Ratio*, 30(1), 1–14.

Malink, M. (2020). Aristotelian demonstration. In M. J. Raven (ed.), *The Routledge Handbook of Metaphysical Grounding*. New York: Routledge, pp. 33–48.

Marmor, A. (2009). *Social Conventions: From Language to Law*. Princeton, NJ: Princeton University Press.

Maurin, A.-S. (2019). Grounding and metaphysical explanation: It's complicated. *Philosophical Studies*, 176(6), 1573–94.

McLaughlin, B. and Bennett, K. (2021). Supervenience. In E. N. Zalta (ed.), *The Stanford Encyclopedia of Philosophy* (online ed., Summer 2021, revised January 10, 2018). https://plato.stanford.edu/archives/sum2021/entries/supervenience/.

McPherson, T. (2018). Authoritatively normative concepts. *Oxford Studies in Metaethics*, 13, 253–77.

McPherson, T. and Plunkett, D. (2017). The nature and explanatory ambitions of metaethics. In T. McPherson and D. Plunkett (eds.), *The Routledge Handbook of Metaethics*. New York: Routledge, pp. 1–25.

McPherson, T. and Plunkett, D. (2024). The fragmentation of authoritative normativity. In R. Shafer-Landau (ed.), *Oxford Studies in Metaethics, Volume 19*. Oxford: Oxford University Press, pp. 1–28.

McPherson, T. and Plunkett, D. (in press). Authoritative normativity. In D. Copp and C. Rosati (eds.), *The Oxford Handbook of Metaethics*. Oxford: Oxford University Press.

Mikkola, M. (2015). Doing ontology and doing justice: What feminist philosophy can teach us about meta-metaphysics. *Inquiry*, 58(7–8), 780–805.

Mikkola, M. (2019). Grounding and anchoring: On the structure of Epstein's social ontology. *Inquiry*, 62(2), 198–216.

Moreso, J. J. (1996). On relevance and justification of legal decisions. *Erkenntnis*, 44(1), 73–100.

Moreso, J. J. (2001). In defense of inclusive legal positivism. In P. Chiassoni (ed.), *The Legal Ought*. Turin: Giappicheli, pp. 37–64.

Moreso, J. J. and Chilovi, S. (2018). Interpretive arguments and the application of the law. In G. Bongiovanni, G. Postema, A. Rotolo, G. Sartor, C. Valentini and D. Walton (eds.), *Handbook of Legal Reasoning and Argumentation*. Dordrecht: Springer, pp. 495–517.

Murphy, L. (2008). Better to see law this way. *New York University Law Review*, 83(4), 1088–108.

Murphy, L. (2014). *What Makes Law: An Introduction to the Philosophy of Law*. New York: Cambridge University Press.

Nye, H. (2022). Does law "exist"? Eliminativism in legal philosophy. *Washington University Jurisprudence Review*, 15(1), 29–78.

Nye, H. (2024). Moral decision-making in the name of society (without expertise). *Jurisprudence*, 15(2), 125–34.

Plunkett, D. (2012). A positivist route for explaining how facts make law. *Legal Theory*, 18(2), 139–207.

Plunkett, D. and Shapiro, S. (2017). Law, morality, and everything else: General jurisprudence as a branch of metanormative inquiry. *Ethics*, 128(1), 37–68.

Plunkett, D., Shapiro, S. J. and Toh, K. (eds.) (2019). *Dimensions of Normativity: New Essays on Metaethics and Jurisprudence*. Oxford: Oxford University Press.

Raven, M. J. (2012). In defence of ground. *Australasian Journal of Philosophy*, 90(4), 687–701.

Raven, M. J. (2013). Is ground a strict partial order? *American Philosophical Quarterly*, 50(2), 193–201.

Raven, M. J. (2015). Ground. *Philosophy Compass*, 10(5), 322–33.

Raven, M. J. (ed.) (2020). *The Routledge Handbook of Metaphysical Grounding*. New York: Routledge.

Raz, J. (1979). *The Authority of Law: Essays on Law and Morality*. Oxford: Oxford University Press.

Rodriguez-Pereyra, G. (2019). Nominalism in metaphysics. In E. N. Zalta (ed.), *The Stanford Encyclopedia of Philosophy* (online ed., Summer 2019, revised April 1, 2015). https://plato.stanford.edu/archives/sum2019/entries/nominalism-metaphysics/.

Rosen, G. (2010). Metaphysical dependence: Grounding and reduction. In B. Hale and A. Hoffmann (eds.), *Modality: Metaphysics, Logic, and Epistemology*. Oxford: Oxford University Press, pp. 109–35.

Rosen, G. (2017a). Ground by law. *Philosophical Issues*, 27, 279–301.
Rosen, G. (2017b). What is a moral law? *Oxford Studies in Metaethics*, 12, 135–59.
Roski, S. (2017). *Bolzano's Conception of Grounding*. Frankfurt: Klostermann.
Roski, S. (2020). Bolzano. In M. J. Raven (ed.), *The Routledge Handbook of Metaphysical Grounding*. New York: Routledge, pp. 76–89.
Schaffer, J. (2009). On what grounds what. In D. Chalmers, D. Manley and R. Wasserman (eds.), *Metametaphysics: New Essays on the Foundations of Ontology*. Oxford: Oxford University Press, pp. 347–83.
Schaffer, J. (2012). Grounding, transitivity, and contrastivity. In F. Correia and B. Schnieder (eds.), *Metaphysical Grounding: Understanding the Structure of Reality*. Cambridge: Cambridge University Press, pp. 122–38.
Schaffer, J. (2016). Grounding in the image of causation. *Philosophical Studies*, 173(1), 49–100.
Schaffer, J. (2017a). The ground between the gaps. *Philosophers' Imprint*, 17, art. 11.
Schaffer, J. (2017b). Laws for metaphysical explanation. *Philosophical Issues*, 27(1), 302–21.
Schaffer, J. (2019). Anchoring as grounding: On Epstein's *The Ant Trap*. *Philosophy and Phenomenological Research*, 99(3), 749–67.
Shapiro, S. J. (2011). *Legality*. Cambridge, MA: Harvard University Press.
Skiles, A. (2015). Against grounding necessitarianism. *Erkenntnis*, 80(4), 717–51.
Srinivasan, A. (2020). Radical externalism. *Philosophical Review*, 129(3), 395–431.
Stavropoulos, N. (1996). *Objectivity in Law*. Oxford: Clarendon Press.
Stavropoulos, N. (2021). Legal interpretivism. In E. N. Zalta (ed.), *The Stanford Encyclopedia of Philosophy* (online ed., Spring 2021, revised February 8, 2021). https://plato.stanford.edu/archives/spr2021/entries/law-interpretivist/.
Tahko, T. E. (2013). Truth-grounding and transitivity. *Thought*, 2(4), 332–40.
Thomasson, A. L. (1998). *Fiction and Metaphysics*. Cambridge: Cambridge University Press.
Thompson, N. (2016). Metaphysical interdependence. In M. Jago (ed.), *Reality Making*. Oxford: Oxford University Press, pp. 38–56.
Torrengo, G. (2018). Nunc pro tunc: The problem of retroactive enactments. *Philosophia*, 46(1), 241–50.
Tripkovic, B. and Patterson, D. (2023). The promise and limits of grounding in law. *Legal Theory*, 29(3), 202–28.
Trogdon, K. (2013a). An introduction to grounding. In B. Schnieder, M. Hoeltje and A. Steinberg (eds.), *Varieties of Dependence: Ontological Dependence, Grounding, Supervenience, Response-Dependence*. Munich: Philosophia, pp. 97–122.

Trogdon, K. (2013b). Grounding: Necessary or contingent? *Pacific Philosophical Quarterly*, 94(4), 465–85.

Waluchow, W. J. (1994). *Inclusive Legal Positivism*. Oxford: Oxford University Press.

Wilsch, T. (2015). The nomological account of ground. *Philosophical Studies*, 172(12), 3293–312.

Wilsch, T. (2016). The deductive-nomological account of metaphysical explanation. *Australasian Journal of Philosophy*, 94(1), 1–23.

Wodak, D. (2019). Mere formalities: Fictional normativity and normative authority. *Canadian Journal of Philosophy*, 49(6), 1–23.

Acknowledgments

For comments on materials from this Element, I'm grateful to audiences at the UCLA Legal Theory Workshop, the UCLA Ethics Workshop, the UCLA Academic Writing Circle, the Social Metaphysics Workshop at UNC Chapel Hill, the 72nd Northwest Philosophy Conference at Portland State University, the Cornell Conference in Legal Philosophy, the Applied Ethics Seminar at the CSIC Institute of Philosophy, the Seminario Permanente de Filosofía del Derecho at Universidad Autónoma de Madrid, the Law and Philosophy Seminar at Universitat Pomepu Fabra, the METIS Research Seminar at UNED, the XXXI IVR World Congress at Soongsil University, the XXV World Philosophy Congress at La Sapienza University of Rome, and the Law and Philosophy Seminar at Glasgow University. For comments on previous drafts, thanks to Thomas Byrne, Brian Epstein, Mark Greenberg, Pamela Hieronymi, Stephan Leuenberger, José Juan Moreso, George Pavlakos, and Seana Shiffrin. Thanks to John Horden for help with the linguistic revision of the text. For their lasting support and invaluable companionship, thanks to Matt Andler, Gloria Andrada, Fernando De los Santos, Begoña Mariezkurrena, Susana Monsó, and Michele Palmira. This publication has been supported by the Ramón y Cajal fellowship "The Metaphysical Structure of Normative Explanation" (grant RYC2021-032064-I funded by MICIU/AEI/ 10.13039/501100011033 and by the European Union NextGenerationEU/PRTR) and by the project "MetaCon – Metanormative Connectedness: On the Relevance of Metanormative Theory for All-Things-Considered Deliberation" (grant PID2023-152006NA-I00 funded by MICIU/AEI/10.13039/501100011033 and by FEDER/UE) based at the Institute of Philosophy (IFS) of the Spanish National Research Council (CSIC).

PID2023-152006NA-I00

RYC2021-032064-I

Cambridge Elements

Philosophy of Law

Series Editors
George Pavlakos
University of Glasgow

George Pavlakos is Professor of Law and Philosophy at the School of Law, University of Glasgow. He has held visiting posts at the universities of Kiel and Luzern, the European University Institute, the UCLA Law School, the Cornell Law School and the Beihang Law School in Beijing. He is the author of *Our Knowledge of the Law* (2007) and more recently has co-edited *Agency, Negligence and Responsibility* (2021) and *Reasons and Intentions in Law and Practical Agency* (2015).

Gerald J. Postema
University of North Carolina at Chapel Hill

Gerald J. Postema is Professor Emeritus of Philosophy at the University of North Carolina at Chapel Hill. Among his publications count *Utility, Publicity, and Law: Bentham's Moral and Legal Philosophy* (2019); *On the Law of Nature, Reason, and the Common Law: Selected Jurisprudential Writings of Sir Matthew Hale* (2017); *Legal Philosophy in the Twentieth Century: The Common Law World* (2011), *Bentham and the Common Law Tradition*, 2nd edition (2019).

Kenneth M. Ehrenberg
University of Surrey

Kenneth M. Ehrenberg is Professor of Jurisprudence and Philosophy at the University of Surrey School of Law and Co-Director of the Surrey Centre for Law and Philosophy. He is the author of *The Functions of Law* (2016) and numerous articles on the nature of law, jurisprudential methodology, the relation of law to morality, practical authority, and the epistemology of evidence law.

Associate Editor
Sally Zhu
University of Sheffield

Sally Zhu is a lecturer in property law at University of Sheffield. Her research is on property and private law aspects of platform and digital economies.

About the Series
This series provides an accessible overview of the philosophy of law, drawing on its varied intellectual traditions in order to showcase the interdisciplinary dimensions of jurisprudential enquiry, review the state of the art in the field, and suggest fresh research agendas for the future. Focussing on issues rather than traditions or authors, each contribution seeks to deepen our understanding of the foundations of the law, ultimately with a view to offering practical insights into some of the major challenges of our age.

Cambridge Elements

Philosophy of Law

Elements in the Series

The Moral Prerequisites of the Criminal Law: Legal Moralism and the Problem of Mala Prohibita
Ambrose Y. K. Lee and Alexander F. Sarch

Legal Personhood
Visa A. J. Kurki

The Philosophy of Legal Proof
Lewis Ross

Content-Independence in Law: Possibility and Potential
Julie Dickson

The Normativity of Law
Michael Giudice

The Nature of Authority
Kenneth Einar Himma

Legal Rights and Moral Rights
Matthew H. Kramer

Dignity and Rights
Ariel Zylberman

Contemporary Non-Positivism
Emad H. Atiq

Subsidiarity
Andreas Follesdal

The Impasse of Constitutional Rights
Jacob Weinrib

The Metaphysics of Legal Facts
Samuele Chilovi

A full series listing is available at: www.cambridge.org/EPHL

For EU product safety concerns, contact us at Calle de José Abascal, 56–1°,
28003 Madrid, Spain or eugpsr@cambridge.org.

www.ingramcontent.com/pod-product-compliance
Lightning Source LLC
LaVergne TN
LVHW011856060526
838200LV00054B/4373